LOVE
IS A
PINK
CAKE
by
corkie & andy

LOVE IS A PINK CAKE:

IRRESISTIBLE BAKES for MORNING, NOON and NIGHT

CLAIRE PTAK

'Love is not only the most important ingredient:
It is the only ingredient which really matters.'
The Tassajara Bread Book

LOVE IS A PINK CAKE

CLAIRE PTAK

W. W. NORTON & COMPANY
Celebrating a Century of Independent Publishing

We bake for love. Whether it's for ourselves, to show love for a child, friend or partner or to celebrate a rite of passage, there is no denying the incredible effect cakes can have. I started baking as a child, taught by my mom and grandma, which is the experience of so many of us. I soon turned my after-school activity into a hobby, which then became a side hustle, as I was always trying to make more money than whatever job I had was paying me. Finally, it became my full-time job and then my career. Now, after nearly two decades of running my own business, Violet Cakes, it still never ceases to amaze me how much impact the gesture of baking a cake for someone can make. In England they use the word 'cake' as an all-encompassing term for sweet baked goods. I adore this use of the word because it's always so positive and often accompanied by a smile. This, my fifth book, is a collection of my current favourites – what I am baking throughout the day, for any occasion. I've always loved the collections of prints *Love Is A Pink Cake* by Andy Warhol, where he looked at different iconic love stories; it is an early project that he self-published. Baking is, in its own way, a love story too.

For Frances

Every morning when I walk my six-year-old daughter Frances to school, we pass Violet, my little California-style bakery in East London. If we have time, we pop in and get a mini banana muffin. If, as is more usual, we're running late, she gets to come after school for a chocolate chip cookie. When she was two, and had sugar for the first time, I decided that I would not obsess about limits and boundaries with food when it is so intrinsically linked to our feelings. Owning a bakery means there is a lot of cake around a lot of the time, but I would let her navigate it, the way my mother and grandmothers did with me.

Even with the choice between cinnamon buns, butterscotch blondies, chocolate devil's food cake or lemon meringue pie bars, Frances says the cakes I make at home taste better than the ones we make at the bakery. Now, I tend to disagree. At the bakery we have a new, state-of-the-art Swedish oven, powerful mixers and the freshest, highest quality ingredients. My bakers work their magic with my recipes, sometimes making them even better than I imagined, through trial and error and daily practice. So I would argue that the cakes in the bakery are better than those I throw together at home; but it isn't the perfection she is talking about. What Frances is tasting, experiencing and appreciating is the love that comes through something made at home, just for her.

The recipes in this book are inspired by my upbringing in Northern California and my new home in London, where I've lived since 2005. Trained at Chez Panisse by Alice Waters, I bake seasonally. First and foremost I go to the market to see what the farmers are growing and then decide what I will bake for my friends or put on the menu at the bakery. My baking is about taking that fresh, fuzzy peach, bloomy plum or crisp apple and playing with the textures and flavours inherent to it, lifting them with salts, sugars, acids, fats and bitterness to make them taste more balanced and more like themselves.

After seasonality and flavour balance comes aesthetic. I studied art and film and I cannot take that critical eye away from anything I do. Even the title of this book has been percolating away in my brain for years. In 1989, when I was 14, I dragged my dad to the Andy Warhol Retrospective at the Art Institute of Chicago when we were there visiting my grandparents. A room of mylar balloons, a silk-screened Chairman Mao and dozens of Marilyn Monroes ignited my imagination. Many years later I discovered one of Warhol's first jobs as a young artist was to illustrate socialite Amy Vanderbilt's *Complete Cookbook*, and from there the collection of prints from which I borrowed the title of this book.

We recently renovated Violet Bakery and replaced the 1940s Hobart mixer with new, better equipment and made more space for our bakers. I wanted Violet to feel even more like a little bit of California in East London. I have loved the Bay Area figurative painter Richard Diebenkorn since high school; his textural brushwork reminds me of frosting. In redecorating the space, I used a colour palette taken from his paintings of the 1970s and 80s. So we have a Diebenkorn blue floor, and accents of yellow set against hues of grey and white, recreating something of California's urban landscapes – the wide streets with buildings so bleached by the sun they become pastel. Wanting Violet to look like that, I filled the space with light and wood, while the cakes provide the colours. Icing colours come from the fresh fruit purées we mix into the butter, the sugar and the cream. Forced rhubarb makes a muted acid pink, roasted plums with their red skins and yellow flesh become a subtle orangey pink; my favourite is when we make a summer pudding compote of blackcurrants, redcurrants, raspberries and loganberries for a fuchsia buttercream – pink is obviously a theme. We always have our signature violet buttercream, which is pale purple in colour, as well as coconut milk, Amalfi lemon and Madagascan vanilla bean, which results in whites and creams.

At nine o'clock on a sunny November morning I was born in Point Reyes Station, a small village in Northern California, above a health food shop that would later become a bakery (when I was 15, I got my first job at that bakery). Named after a former train stop, Point Reyes Station is one of eight small villages – alongside Muir Beach, Stinson Beach, Bolinas, Olema, Inverness, Marshall and Tomales – collectively referred to as West Marin. Highway 1 runs through the main street and then takes you south along the coast to San Francisco in an hour.

My parents moved there and eventually to the neighbouring town, Inverness, in the 1970s and helped found a small theatre company. Alongside a whole troupe of artists, musicians and hippies, they made their home on the edge of Point Reyes National Seashore. Mom made costumes and wrote scripts; Dad directed plays. They thrived in this wild, free-loving community. There was lots of love, and yes, lots of drugs and some casualties. But its radical spirit and artistry lives on.

As a teenager growing up in the middle of all this, I was rebelliously keen on making money. The Bovine Bakery was my first 'official' job. Before that I had swept the front porch at a gift shop and cleaned the rooms and made bran muffins for a bed & breakfast. My mom also had a children's clothing outlet – the samples for the designs she sold in Saks Fifth Avenue. I hung out there every day after school. I often think about the unintentional parallels between mine and my daughter's childhoods.

As well as these three jobs, I did some other formative work, although I wouldn't come to fully understand its influence until years later when I began to write this book. A handful of times, I separated clay for Rick Yoshimoto, the former assistant to local sculptor JB Blunk, and a prolific artist in his own right. As a child I knew JB less as a celebrated artist than as my friend Mariah's dad, the guy who made the crazy wedding cake at the beginning of this introduction for Rick and Suzanne. It took half a dozen people to carry the landscape of cake, dripping in white and pink icing with erect dyed-blue bananas, cross sections of seeded papaya and inside-out sliced mangoes across the lawn, squealing children swarming around the table while the adults exchanged knowing glances and smiles. The theatre and artistry of this cake impressed me enormously – not just the cake itself but everyone's reactions to it. The love-energy swirling around the big reveal of this cake was contagious. I knew I wanted to create in this way when I grew up.

The work I did for Rick was not at all exciting, but I could tell it was important. Standing at a hand-crafted table piled high with freshly dug-up earth from the Inverness Ridge where we lived, I spent hours using a small pick to separate usable clay from unusable dirt. That first experience of separating natural clay was the beginning of an adolescence informed by the landscape, and the beginning of a career informed by a sense of home and place and grounded in a love of what you do. Little did I know that some 35 years later I would be returning home to the town of Inverness, California from East London to photograph my fifth cookbook in JB Blunk's hand-built home. Even less could I imagine that during that shoot I would come to understand something about the parallels between his sculptural, artistic process and the work I do now. He became friends with the renowned artist and landscape architect Isamu Noguchi, whose retrospective I would later see that

fall at the Barbican back in London. JB was featured in a video in the exhibition. I found myself thinking about JB and Noguchi's work and the fact that cooking, like sculpture, is about taking a natural shape, material or ingredient and making it better by making it more itself.

I stayed at the Blunk House for a week with my photographer Maren Caruso and my assistant chef Siew Chin in the balmy autumn of 2021. Siew and I had worked together 20 years earlier at Chez Panisse, so it was a homecoming of more than one sort. When we first slid open the heavy redwood door, I had no idea how much the space would inform the shoot. The small wooden kitchen overlooks a bishop pine forest cooled by rolling fog. The landscape reminded me to stay true to the vital simplicity of the ingredients it produces, and that less is always more. As I baked up there on the ridge, I adjusted some of the recipes to make them simpler, stopping always when I realised 'this is enough'. At the same time, I felt more aware than ever of the collaborative nature of my work.

Each morning we would meet in the kitchen at 6 a.m., make a small pot of coffee, eat whatever cake was left from the day before and discuss the plan for the day ahead. We were trying to fit in about ten shots a day, which alongside baking is really quite a lot. We usually finished shooting when we lost the light around 6 p.m., and then spent the next few hours prepping recipes for the following day. Yes. We were working 15 hours a day, but it didn't feel like work. I can honestly say we loved every minute of it.

As we cooked, my family and friends delivered the best produce of the season. Mom brought quince she'd picked that morning from her friend's tree; Dad brought bouquets of wild fennel for their fragrant yellow pollen; a huge crate of Meyer lemons arrived from a friend; and neighbours collected gallons of wild huckleberries from the woods. We had also visited Frog Hollow Farm the day before at sunrise to pick peaches and take photographs. After all the cakes were shot we would call these friends back to come and take home the bakes that their gifts had become.

This seasonality and sense of place is at the heart of what makes me a Californian baker, and the slice of home I have brought with me to London and to Violet. You can't get those same ingredients here that you can in California, but the English countryside has its own storybook offering: gooseberries, jostaberries, redcurrants, whitecurrants, blackcurrants and loganberries. Yorkshire forced rhubarb is another gift of England that even has Protected Designation of

LOVE IS A PINK CAKE

Origin. I have always looked for a way to adapt the approach I grew up with, finding a marriage of two worlds: pairing English ingredients with a Californian sensibility. Maybe that is part of the reason Meghan Markle and Prince Harry chose me to make their wedding cake and their daughter Lilibet's 1st birthday cake: a lemon-elderflower cake iced with pink strawberry buttercream. We make so many wedding cakes, birthday cakes and cakes to mark triumphs and accomplishments in people's lives. Some are ordered as gifts, some are carefully decided upon together and some are just for the buyer. One of my favourite-ever messages we stamped out on our signature paper banners was 'Happy birthday to me'. I mean, what a fantastic act of self-love!

To get the produce I wanted for the English part of this book, we drove for six hours to Fern Verrow Farm in Herefordshire. We photographed Jane's Secret-Garden-like farm, loaded the back of my car with the booty and drove it all back to Columbia Road, in London's East End, with its historic flower market and Victorian architecture, to bake with for this book. My friend Ruthie Rogers talks about ingredients being the 'poetry of what you might be cooking'. This idea really resonates with me as someone who cares so much about the ingredients we are starting with and why I have made the effort to seek out these amazing producers.

I found a way to do what I love for a living. My life and work are deeply connected. I came to realise something else about my own work. That the art of baking is as much in the practice and process as in the result. It's the doing of it, every day. The repetitive, embodied creativity. As a child I came home from school and baked. I baked for myself and I baked for the people I loved. I rarely go to someone's house or to a meeting without some cakes in tow. I think the reason my career has grown more than I could ever have imagined – from running a market stall out of the back of my car, to opening Violet, to baking 'that' wedding cake – is by keeping my focus narrow, with a few very specific non-negotiables: to use the best possible ingredients, to make flavour more important than form and, most of all, doing the work.

The other morning, after dropping off my daughter at school I was walking back to Violet, going over the day's to do list in my mind. Just as I reached the corner of Wilton Way and Greenwood Road I saw a slightly broken branch of a cherry tree that had spilled its blossoms all over the parked cars below. Broken, but beautiful. I love this time of year when the trees outside the bakery are a cloud of pink. Of course I dream of California, with its warm air and perfect produce, but London pulled me in, grabbed hold, challenged me and transformed me. My perspective is different from the one I moved here with. After nearly two decades in Hackney, my California baking has a different point of view. Take the experience of your life and let it shape your baking. Bake more often. Bake for those you love. Love is a pink cake.

LOVE IS A PINK CAKE

ON MEASUREMENTS

At Violet we weigh everything, including liquids, and I suggest you do this at home too. If you haven't got one already, I recommend you invest in a small set of digital kitchen scales.

While I have done all the conversions for you (adding cups in parentheses) I've included my conversion chart at the end of the book, on page 259. It may be useful for other books you have, or for recipes from the internet. The key thing to remember is that ingredients vary greatly in volume depending on texture, density, viscosity and grain or granule size. For example, a cup of sugar weighs 200g but a cup of plain (all-purpose) flour weighs 140g. Cup conversions are not interchangeable.

ON LANGUAGE

Because this book was written by an American who has spent the last 18 years in England, there are some funny inconsistencies in its language. The way I now spell flavour with a 'u', weigh out all my ingredients in grams, call it semi-skimmed milk rather than low-fat; but a cookie is never a biscuit. I have decided to add a little glossary here to help American readers, rather than Americanise the text.

UK	US
Strong flour	Bread flour
Soft brown sugar	Brown sugar
Cake tin	Cake pan
Caster sugar	Super-fine/ granulated sugar
Clingfilm	Plastic wrap
Double cream	Heavy cream
Icing sugar	Confectioner's/ powdered sugar
Plain flour	All-purpose flour
Pudding	Dessert
Semi-skimmed milk	Low-fat milk
Single cream	Half and half
Tin	Can
Wholemeal	Whole wheat

ON FORAGING

I grew up foraging in California, which I discuss in a bit more detail in *The Violet Bakery Cookbook*. I highly recommend foraging to all bakers. The leaves, blossoms and berries of many trees that grow in cities and along country roads can greatly improve the complexity of your baking, making it hyper seasonal. Wherever I go in the world, I keep an eye out for plants that I can use in my baking – just in case! I love to cook when I travel, never missing a trip to the markets to see what is available. This includes pulling over on the roadside in Italy for a few fig leaves to add to a custard or picking wild strawberries in the forest in France. I snag rosehips growing near the canals in East London to add to plum jam; and I'm always out grabbing nettles (gloved, of course) for quiches and frittatas. Blackberries and fennel flowers grow just about everywhere in England and California, but find out what grows where you live. Get a book or an app to always make sure you identify wild plants with caution and care as they can be poisonous.

Some ingredients in this book, like peach leaves, may be difficult to forage (or borrow), especially if you don't happen to know someone with a walled garden or orchard. But go to your local farmer's market and ask the peach farmers to bring you a couple of branches the following week. Don't be shy; the worst thing they can say is no.

GROW HERBS

On my terrace in London I grow rose geranium and lemon verbena along with, of course, the usual suspects: mint, oregano, rosemary and thyme. A few of these leaves in roasted fruits, custards, jams or sauces transform a dish and make it extra special. It feels good to go outside and spend a minute or two with the bees.

UNDERDO
RATHER THAN OVERDO

Under-whip cream. You can always go back with a hand whisk and whip a little more, but you can't bring it back once it turns into butter. Remember that you will most likely be scooping the cream onto a plate or a whole cake, and even that action is essentially churning the cream more. Scraping down the sides with a spatula does the same thing, so leave it a little under to allow for these extra turns that will inevitably take place. If it is just a little too thick, but not curdled, a splash of fresh cream gently folded through can bring it back.

Under-whip egg whites. All my recipes that call for eggs to be separated, whipped up and folded back together will have an amount of sugar in both the whites *and* the yolks. The sugar gives the whites structure and stability and makes the folding-together process much easier. I prefer to under-whip so you don't get those bitty, broken whites that leave white specks in your cake mixture. When the whites are the same texture as the mixture they are being folded into (i.e. dropping or ribboning off a spoon rather than being stiff and broken) they will incorporate beautifully. The only time I go super stiff is when making marshmallow or meringue, but there is *so* much sugar in those recipes that it's virtually impossible to over-whip.

Under-work dough. For biscuits, scones and pastry, remember to let the doughs rest and let time do the work. You are trying to get the dry ingredients to absorb the wet. Over-working will only make the end result tough. Sometimes it seems like an impossible amount of dry ingredients for the smaller amount of wet, but do not be hasty and add extra wet or go wild trying to mix it all together into a ball. After 5–10 minutes of rest, you will notice a marked difference in the tenderness of your dough. It's something only time can achieve.

Don't over-blanche leaves. When steeping peach or fig leaves in warm milk or cream, be sure to do it quickly, multiple times, with fresh leaves. This keeps not only the colour but the flavour bright and green. Over-steeping can make the taste vegetal and unappealing.

One place where the under-doing rule does not apply is when creaming butter and sugar for a cake, or butter and icing sugar for a buttercream. In that instance I would, in the words of my grandmother Betty, 'Beat like mad!'

FREEZING with INTENTION
Freezing gets a bad rap. What was a post-war game-changer for many households became synonymous with processed frozen foods, and a freezer was certainly something you wanted to downplay the use of in artisanal food businesses. But freezers can help tremendously for more uniformity in your baking and with good organisation. Scones baked from frozen look great and, of course, you can bake a batch of scones that have been frozen overnight first thing in the morning and delight your guests and family with the smell of baking pastries as they wake up.

Cookie dough can be frozen until the next time you need it. Who doesn't prefer a warm, crisp on the outside, gooey on the inside chocolate-chip cookie to a slightly floppy, stuck together one out of a container from a day or two before? Of course, there is a place for a cookie tin or jar; but better to put crisp cookies into those – what the English call biscuits.

TAP YOUR TINS
Once you have portioned your cake mixtures into prepared tins, I like to give them a good tap on the counter to release any large air bubbles before they go into the oven.

Tap trays of cookies once baked, while still hot, to flatten them slightly and expose pools of melted chocolate. Remember, cookies always look under-baked, but they will continue to bake a little more as they cool and eventually set. This is how you get that perfect texture of crisp on the outside and gooey on the inside.

SALTED, NOT SALTY
I work with many different salts, choosing them for a particular recipe based on colour, texture or provenance. There is a real trend in baking to use a lot of salt, and while I think salt is essential in most recipes to achieve balance, be careful not to be heavy-handed. Don't forget to taste the batter, dough or mixture just as you would with savoury cooking, to make sure the balance of flavour has been achieved. Remember that a little salt in baking is meant to cut sweetness and bring out subtle flavours in fruit, chocolate, caramel, etc. The finishing flakes of salt on a cookie should enhance it, not overwhelm.

All salt is basically chemically the same (unless iodised), but it's the texture and the way it hits your tastebuds, dissolves, and incorporates into a recipe that make various salts drastically different from one another. I bake with fine sea salt, which is saltier than kosher salt, so if you use kosher, add a little pinch more. For finishing, I often use flakes, but I also have a mortar and pestle in my kitchen that is specifically for pounding coarser salts into finer crystals. My drawer at home has up to ten salts at any one time: flaky sea salt from Halen Môn or Maldon for chocolate chip cookies; sel de Guérande for bread; sel gris and fleur de sel for matcha blondies; and black and pink Himalayan salts for decoration, plus a pretty, peachy-coloured salt from Australia and an old-fashioned table salt for good measure. I always love how the tables at Zuni Café in San Francisco have a great big glass saltshaker of table salt. So chic.

EQUIPMENT
I highly recommend having the following essentials in your baking kitchen to make life easier as well as yield the best results:
- Cling film for decorating cakes – while I have pretty much got rid of plastic everywhere else in the kitchen, I have not found a better method of layering and decorating cakes then to line a cake tin with cling film
- Spider strainer – for poaching peaches
- Pastry cutter – for making biscuits
- Ice-cream scoops – for perfectly portioning cookies

- Stand mixer – when a recipe calls for a mixer you can use a stand mixer or a hand-held mixer, but a stand mixer has a stronger motor and you can leave it to whip egg whites or other ingredients while you get on with something else
- Bench scraper – for cutting scones and cleaning down sticky counters
- Cooking spray – much quicker for greasing cake tins evenly
- Baking tins – have a good selection of baking tins, preferably anodised aluminium with loose bottoms

INGREDIENTS

I always say 'I'm just a really good shopper' when people say how much they like my cooking. It doesn't mean I'm not a good cook, it is just to highlight that delicious food starts with delicious ingredients, seeking out the best chocolates, freshest flours, and of course perfectly ripe seasonal produce.

Butter is always unsalted and European for a higher fat content.

Eggs are always large (about 60g once shelled) and free-range.

At the bakery we use many specialty items, such as a French violet syrup (not to be confused with violet liqueur or violet extract). Most specialty items can be found online, and there are a few specialty chef sites that I like to use. Think of all the different specialty forms of vanilla available: pods, pastes, extracts, essences, powders. Each one has a different concentration and flavour. So do your best to use what is called for in the recipe or make adjustments accordingly.

CALIF

MORNINGS

BLACK TEA
POPPY SEED MUFFINS

Poppy seed muffins are a classic breakfast muffin in America but often just taste of lemon. Soaking poppy seeds in black tea releases their floral flavour while activating the availability of their nutrition, transforming the flavour of this muffin. Welcome to the wonderful world of poppy seeds.

Makes 6 large muffins

50g (½ cup) poppy seeds, soaked
    in 60g (¼ cup) brewed black tea
    overnight or for at least 2 hours
280g (2 cups) white spelt flour
50g (½ cup) ground almonds
2 tsp baking powder
½ tsp fine sea salt
115g (1 stick or ½ cup) unsalted
    butter, softened
150g (¾ cup) caster sugar,
    plus more for sprinkling
2 tbsp honey
2 eggs
120g (½ cup) whole milk
Zest and juice of 1 Meyer lemon,
    pink lemon or bergamot lemon

Baker's tip: Bergamot lemons are used to make Earl Grey tea so you could soak the poppy seeds in Earl Grey to add another more nuanced layer of citrus flavour to these already citrussy muffins.

1. Preheat the oven to 180°C fan/200°C/ 400°F/gas mark 6. Grease the top of a large muffin or cupcake tray and line it with 6 paper muffin cases. Space the cases out, using every other cup.

2. In a large bowl, whisk together the spelt flour, ground almonds, baking powder and salt. Set aside.

3. In the bowl of a stand mixer, cream the softened butter, sugar and honey together until light and fluffy. Add the eggs one at a time, mixing well after each addition. Add the soaked poppy seeds and any of their liquid and stir to combine.

4. Add half of the dry mixture to the butter mixture and mix until combined, then add the milk, lemon zest and juice and mix again. Finally add the remainder of the dry mixture just until incorporated.

5. Scoop the mixture into the paper cases (they will be quite full) and sprinkle the tops generously with caster sugar.

6. Bake for 20–30 minutes, or until golden and springy to the touch. Serve with lemon curd or another favourite preserve.

BLACKBERRY and ROSE WALNUT CRUMBLE CAKE

This recipe is loosely inspired by the flavours in one of my favourite sweets, Ma'amoul, a plump buttery semolina cookie filled with walnuts, rose water and cinnamon, traditionally made and eaten in the Arab world at the end of a day of fasting during the holy month of Ramadan. London-based Lebanese chef Anissa Helou showed me how to make these delicious cookies with moulds passed down to her from her Syrian grandmother. So good with a coffee, I transformed them into a breakfast cake.

Serves 8–12

150g (5½oz) almond paste
 (at least 50% almonds)
115g (1 stick or ½ cup) unsalted
 butter, softened
½ tsp sea salt
100g (½ cup) caster sugar
2 eggs
1 tsp vanilla extract
210g (1½ cups) plain flour
1¼ tsp baking powder
½ tsp bicarbonate soda
250g (1¼ cups) plain yoghurt (not
 strained or Greek)
200g (1¼ cups) blackberries
 fresh or frozen

For the crumble:
100g (¾ cup) fine semolina flour
¼ tsp sea salt
70g (5 tbsp) chilled unsalted
 butter, cut into 1cm (½in) pieces
100g (½ cup) walnuts, finely chopped
2 tbsp rose water
1 tsp ground cinnamon
50g (¼ cup) caster sugar

1. Preheat the oven to 160°C fan/180°C/ 350°F/gas mark 4. Butter and line a 23×33cm (9×13in) cake tin with baking paper.

2. First make the crumble mixture. Put all the ingredients into a food processor and pulse to combine. Chill until ready to use.

3. In the bowl of an electric mixer, beat the almond paste, butter, salt and sugar until light and fluffy. Add the eggs and vanilla and beat well.

4. In a small bowl, weigh out the flour, baking powder and bicarb and whisk together well. Add to the butter mixture and mix until smooth. Add the yoghurt and mix until just combined. Scrape the bowl and mix one last time.

5. Tip half the mixture into the prepared tin and sprinkle with the blackberries and half the crumble topping. Cover with the other half of the batter and top with the remaining crumble mixture. Bake for 35–40 minutes, or until a skewer inserted in the centre comes out clean.

6. Serve warm or room temperature – it's best eaten the same day.

OASIS DATE SHAKE
(VGN, GF)

This started as a shake inspired by a trip to an oasis between Palm Springs and Joshua Tree in Southern California, where date palms sway heavy in the dawn heat. The allure of a roadside date shake was too strong to pass up, but the shake was way too sweet and not for me. So I came up with this recipe, for a smoothie I actually want to drink. I adore dates. Medjools are king, but try other varieties such as the smaller gooey Barhi or Iranian dates.

Serves 2

8–10 ripe Iranian or
    Barhi dates, pitted
2 medium bananas
    (preferably pre-frozen)
180g (¾ cup) unsweetened
    almond milk
2 tbsp crunchy peanut butter
1 tsp vanilla extract
200g (1 cup) coconut yoghurt
1 tbsp cacao nibs
A couple of ice cubes
Pinch of salt

1. Put everything in a blender, blitz to a smooth purée and drink right away.

FIG TARTLETS
with CRUSHED ALMOND FRANGIPANE

One very hungover morning in Paris after a late night sampling the best *apéro* spots with friends, I dragged myself out of bed to Du Pain et des Idées and bought a fig pastry that quite literally saved my life. This is my version – made with puff pastry instead of croissant dough. If you have the time and the gumption to make puff pastry from scratch, I've included my baker friend Siew Chin's brilliant recipe on page 253. Alternatively, there are so many good quality all-butter puff pastry products on the market, you should not feel guilty just buying one.

Makes 6 tartlets

500g (1lb 2oz) puff pastry
  (see page 253)
18 small to medium ripe figs
6 tbsp caster sugar
Icing sugar, for dusting

For the frangipane:
100g (½ cup) whole almonds, skins on
115g (1 stick or ½ cup) unsalted
  butter, softened
125g (scant ¾ cup) caster sugar
4 egg yolks
4 tsp double cream
1 tbsp kirsch (optional)

1. Roll out your puff pastry to a thickness of about 4mm (⅛ in). Cut six 15cm (6in) oval discs and place them on a couple of baking trays lined with baking paper. Chill or freeze until ready to use.

2. Finely chop the almonds with a sharp knife. You can also use a food processor, but don't let the nuts become so fine they start to release their oils; they should remain dry and powdery. Beat the butter and sugar together in a large bowl until pale and fluffy. Add the egg yolks and combine, then add the almonds and beat well. Add the cream and kirsch (if using). Mix until everything is combined and set aside.

3. Preheat the oven to 200°C fan/220°C/425°F/gas mark 7.

4. Remove the pastry discs from the fridge or freezer and spread each one with 2 heaped tablespoons of the frangipane. Trim off the tough stalks of the figs, retaining as much of the nice curve of the fig as possible. Slice the figs into quarters from top to tail and arrange, slightly overlapping, on the frangipane. Sprinkle a tablespoon of caster sugar over each tart and bake for 30–35 minutes, or until puffed and golden and the fruit is bubbly and starting to caramelise on top.

5. Cool slightly and dust with icing sugar. Serve warm if possible, but they are lovely at room temperature as well.

HUCKLEBERRY BASIL SUGAR SCONES

This beautiful recipe for basil sugar comes from my friend Thalia Ho, a talented Australian baker I met in Paris. I'm in love with all of her recipes, mostly because of her love of bold flavours and her poetic palate. Huckleberries are a wild blueberry that grows in the forests of North America. They are very small and time-consuming to pick and clean, but their deep woodsy flavour makes it worth it. Plus they are the bear's favourite snack. If you don't have huckleberries you can use blueberries instead.

Makes 8 scones

For the basil sugar:
100g (½ cup) caster sugar
20g (¼ cup) fresh basil leaves

For the scones:
100g (½ cup) caster sugar
385g (2¾ cups) plain flour,
  plus more for dusting
1 tbsp baking powder
¾ tsp bicarbonate soda
½ tsp salt
115g (1 stick or ½ cup) unsalted
  butter, chilled
300g (2½ cups) crème fraîche
  or sour cream
200g (1½ cups) huckleberries
  or blueberries
1 egg or egg yolk, beaten with
  a little milk or cream

1. Start with the basil sugar: pulse the sugar and basil leaves in a food processor into a sandy mixture and set aside.

2. In a medium bowl, combine the sugar, flour, baking powder, bicarbonate of soda and salt. Cut in the cold butter with a pastry cutter or the back of a fork (or use a stand mixer) until you have a crumbly mixture. Mix in the crème fraîche until a shaggy dough forms. Gently mix in the huckleberries and turn out onto a floured surface.

3. Pat the dough out into an 18cm (7in) square. Sprinkle with the basil sugar (it may be quite wet but that's ok).

4. Fold the dough in half like a book, to enclose the sugar. Flatten back down to about 5cm (2in) thick, then fold in half once again and pat into a thick square, dusting with additional flour if needed. Cut into quarters so that you have 4 squares and then cut each square in half, so you have 8 triangle shapes.

5. Freeze the dough for at least 30 minutes, or chill in the fridge for about an hour. (You can also freeze the triangles in a sealed container and bake them off as and when you need them.)

6. Preheat the oven to 180°C fan/200°C/ 400°F/gas mark 6 and line a large baking sheet with baking paper.

7. Place the chilled scones on the lined baking sheet and brush with the egg wash. Bake for 25–30 minutes, or until golden.

WHOLE WHEAT
AMERICAN BISCUITS

I love fluffy biscuits (similar to a scone, and definitely not a cookie) and am always trying to perfect them. I love to try different flours and I go back and forth between buttermilk and plain yoghurt for the best tang. These came from wanting to get more whole grains into my and my daughter's diet, but also because I think the rich flavour of whole wheat loves butter. Serve warm with lashings of salty fresh butter, preferably cultured, and a good jam.

Makes 6 biscuits

175g (1¼ cups) plain flour,
    plus more for rolling out
175g (1¼ cups) wholemeal flour
1 tbsp baking powder
1½ tsp fine sea salt
115g (1 stick or ½ cup) unsalted butter,
    cold and cut into 1cm (½in) cubes
400g (1½ cups + 2 tbsp) plain yoghurt
    (not Greek)

1. Preheat the oven to 200°C fan/220°C/ 425°F/gas mark 7 and line a baking sheet with baking paper.

2. In a large bowl, whisk together the flours, baking powder and the salt. Using a pastry cutter or round-bladed knife, cut the butter into the flour mixture until the butter is roughly the size of pepper-corns. Stir in the yoghurt quickly until it comes together into a raggedy ball. It will be a bit wet and sticky but this is what you are going for.

3. Transfer the dough to a lightly floured work surface and press or roll into a square about 3cm (1¼in) thick. Use a 7cm (2¾in) floured, round cutter to stamp out 6 biscuits. Flouring the cutter keeps the sides from getting pinched which would inhibit the rise. You want a nice straight clean cut.

4. Arrange the biscuits on the lined baking sheet so they are almost touching each other and pierce with a fork. As they bake they will push each other up into fluffy biscuits.

5. Bake for about 15–20 minutes until the tops are golden and the biscuits are cooked through. Serve within a few hours of making.

FROG HOLLOW FARM: an ORGANIC FRUIT FARM in NORTHERN CALIFORNIA

Working for Alice Waters at Chez Panisse meant building relationships with the farmers whose produce we cooked. Whether it was at the back door of the pastry kitchen, where stone fruits, citruses, apples and fresh dates were stacked up in colourful boxes, or at the farmer's market, where we went on our days off to shop for our own dinner parties, talking to the farmers was a highlight. These people, who are so deeply connected to the rhythm of the seasons and to the patterns of the plants they grow are, to me, operating on a higher vibrational frequency, more peaceful, more serene.

Frog Hollow Farm was one of the very first farms I was introduced to at the restaurant. So of course it was one of the first places I wanted to include in this book. On my first morning back in California for the photoshoot, we travelled to the farm at 4 a.m. to get the produce for the recipes we would bake for this cookbook. We drove in the dark to reach the farm in time for the golden hour – when the sun is at just the right level to make everything golden. Later, once the sun had risen, we walked through organic peach and plum orchards alongside the farm's founder, Farmer Al, and the pickers, who were all trying to beat the day's heat. Farmer Al grew up in the Bay Area and has run his 253-acre farm since the 1970s. Ever curious and always thinking ahead, his business has been so successful because of his contagious passion for growing delicious fruits and vegetables. Al is a family guy, who chose the farming life to be close to his family every day. An organic and regenerative farm, they work tirelessly to build climate resilience by nurturing healthy soil. The dropped fruit becomes the most beautiful piles of compost you have ever seen. This supports the health of the farm's ecosystem as well as the health of the humans who work on it. We could see this that morning as the crews moved quickly and efficiently through the orchards, singing and laughing with us in that golden light, moments before a light shower of rain, which resulted in a rainbow just above the horizon.

AFTERNOONS

BIG SUR COOKIES

This cookie came out of a mishap at the bakery. A new baker made an enormous batch of granola but added the dried fruit to the mixture while the toasted granola was still warm. The result was a soft granola rather than a crunchy one. So rather than lose it, we turned it into what became my new favourite cookie. It was a great reminder of how mistakes can become triumphs and are always a learning experience. The name comes from one of my favourite places in California, the coastal town of Big Sur which, for whatever reason, I associate with granola.

Makes 18 cookies

150g (1 cup) wholemeal flour
140g (1 cup) plain flour
1½ tsp baking powder
1 tsp fine sea salt
225g (2 sticks or 1 cup) unsalted
   butter, softened
135g (⅔ cup) soft light brown sugar
2 eggs
1 tsp vanilla extract
200g (7oz) white chocolate, chopped
   into chunks
400g (3¼ cups) granola (your favourite
   store-bought or homemade)
Flaky sea salt, for sprinkling

1. Whisk the flours, baking powder and salt together and set aside.

2. Cream the butter and brown sugar just until smooth and combined but do not aerate or make fluffy.

3. Add the eggs and vanilla extract and mix well, then mix in the flour until just combined.

4. Add the white chocolate and granola and mix again, just until it all comes together.

5. Line 1 or 2 baking sheets with baking paper, then use an ice-cream scoop to portion out 18 balls of cookie dough onto the baking sheets. Chill for 30 minutes, then flatten to a thickness of 1.5cm (½in) and freeze.

6. Preheat the oven to 170°C fan/190°C/375°F/gas mark 5.

7. Defrost the cookies for 5–10 minutes before baking. Sprinkle with the flaky sea salt and bake for 7–10 minutes. They should be just starting to colour, but still soft in the centre.

BLONDE PEANUT BUTTER COOKIES

This is the perfect peanut butter cookie. The small amount of wholemeal flour adds a chewiness to the cookie and the lemon juice adds a little acidity to balance the richness. I only recently discovered blonde chocolate – caramelised white chocolate – and it's perfect in peanut butter cookies where I find dark chocolate too bitter.

Makes 12 cookies

115g (1 stick) unsalted butter
250g (1¼ cups) soft light brown sugar
155g (5½oz) crunchy peanut butter
1 egg
1 tsp lemon juice
1½ tsp vanilla extract
100g (¾ cup) plain flour
75g (½ cup) wholemeal flour
½ tsp baking powder
½ tsp fine sea salt
150g (5½oz) blonde chocolate or white chocolate, chopped
Flaky sea salt, for sprinkling

Baker's tip: If you can't find blonde chocolate, you can bake white chocolate (at least 30% cocoa solids) in the oven at 100°C fan/120°C/250°F/gas ½, stirring every 15 minutes until golden and nutty. Spread into a tray to set, then break up and use as chips.

1. In the bowl of a stand mixer fitted with the paddle attachment, cream the butter, sugar and peanut butter together. Add the egg, lemon juice and vanilla and beat well.

2. Whisk together the flours, baking powder and sea salt in a separate bowl, then add these dry ingredients to the butter and egg mixture along with the chocolate and mix until combined.

3. Scoop individual portions of cookie dough onto a tray. If using spoons, pat each portion into a little ball then flatten to about 2.5cm (1in) thick. Use a fork dipped in water and press the tines down into the tops of the cookies in a hashtag pattern. Cover and chill or freeze for at least 1 hour. (You can bake them straightaway, but the cookies will be slightly flatter, or freeze them for up to a month, baking off as and when you want them.)

4. When you are ready to bake, preheat the oven to 170°C fan/190°C/375°F/gas mark 5 and line a large baking sheet with baking paper. If you are baking from frozen, allow the cookies 5–10 minutes out of the freezer before placing in the oven. Arrange the cookies evenly on the sheet, leaving enough space between each one so they have room to expand during baking.

5. Sprinkle with a small amount of flaky sea salt and bake for 8–10 minutes until the centre of each cookie is slightly soft and underbaked but the edges are turning crisp and golden. Remove from the oven and allow to cool on the tray for 5–10 minutes before enjoying.

RYE BROWN BUTTER CHOCOLATE CHIP COOKIES

I love the nuttiness of brown butter and cookies are a great way to use this technique because the flavour really shines through. I have been baking with rye flour for many years because of its unique flavour and chewy texture. It's very heavy though so I prefer to mix it with some plain flour too. I always add a fair amount of salt to cookies for good flavour balance. Grey salt has coarse texture and crunch that can really stand up to and complement the bitter rye flour.

Makes 18 cookies

225g (2 sticks or 1 cup) unsalted butter
200g (1½ cups) wholemeal rye flour
175g (1¼ cups) plain flour
1 tsp fine sea salt
1 tsp baking powder
1¼ tsp bicarbonate of soda
350g (1¾ cups) soft light brown sugar
2 egg yolks
1 tbsp vanilla extract
5 tbsp sweetened condensed milk
250g (9oz) dark milk chocolate
    (40% cocoa solids)
Grey salt, for sprinkling

Baker's tip: Using melted butter in this recipe means that you can stir the mixture by hand, if you don't have an electric whisk or stand mixer.

1. In a small saucepan over a medium heat, melt the butter until it starts to sizzle and foam. The white milk solids should settle to the bottom of the pan and start to turn golden brown (if it goes black, you have gone too far and must start again). Swirl the pan a few more times then remove from the heat to cool slightly.

2. Weigh out the flours, salt, baking powder and bicarbonate soda and set aside.

3. In the bowl of a stand mixer fitted with the paddle attachment, beat the brown butter (including any brown bits from the bottom of the pan) and sugar until well mixed. You can also mix by hand with a wooden spoon.

4. Add the egg yolks, vanilla and condensed milk and mix well. Scrape down the bowl and mix again, then add the flour and mix until just combined. Finally mix in the chocolate chips.

5. Line a couple of baking sheets with baking paper. Use an ice-cream scoop to portion 18 cookies into a container that fits into your fridge or freezer. Chill or freeze for at least 30 minutes – towards the end of the chilling time preheat the oven to 170°C fan/190°C/375°F/gas mark 5.

6. Place the amount of cookies you want to bake onto a lined baking sheet, spaced apart as they will almost double in size. Finish the cookies with a sprinkle of grey salt and bake in the oven for 10–12 minutes. Cool slightly before eating.

VEGAN CHOCOLATE CHIP COOKIES (VGN)

A chewy, gooey chocolate chip cookie that is totally plant-based and totally delicious. I wanted to create a chocolate chip cookie for our vegan friends that was as good as our beloved egg yolk chocolate chip cookies. In other words, a cookie for vegans with plenty of sugar and white flour! Not all vegans want healthy bakes, so this one is for them.

Makes 18 cookies

1 tbsp ground flaxseeds
60g (¼ cup) oat milk
455g (3¼ cups) plain flour
60g (½ cup) rolled oats
1¼ tsp baking powder
1 tsp bicarbonate of soda
1 tsp fine sea salt
250g (1 cup + 2 tbsp) plant-based butter
250g (1¼ cups) soft light brown sugar
150g (¾ cup) caster sugar
1 tsp vanilla extract
250g (9oz) vegan chocolate, broken
    into 1cm (½in) pieces
Flaky sea salt, to finish

1. Soak the ground flaxseeds in the oat milk and set aside.

2. Whisk together the flour, oats, baking powder, bicarb and salt in a bowl and set aside.

3. In the bowl of a stand mixer fitted with the paddle attachment, beat the vegan butter and both sugars until creamy. Beat in the flax mixture and vanilla, then add the dry ingredients and mix until just combined. Finally add the chocolate and mix once again.

4. Use and ice-cream scoop to portion out 18 cookies onto a tray. Chill or freeze for at least 1 hour. (You can also store the unbaked cookies in the freezer and bake as needed.)

5. When ready to bake, preheat the oven to 170°C fan/190°C/375°F/gas mark 5. Line 1 or 2 large baking sheets with baking paper and arrange the dough evenly on the trays, leaving enough space between each one so they have room to expand during baking (they almost double in size). If you are baking from frozen, allow the cookies 5 minutes out of the freezer before placing in the oven.

6. Sprinkle a few flakes of sea salt over the top of each cookie and then bake for 12–14 minutes until the centre of each cookie is slightly soft and underbaked but the edges are crisp and golden. Remove from the oven and allow to cool on the tray for 10 minutes before eating.

My friend Mustafa, an angelic singer and poet from Canada, was recording in London when we met. Mustafa loves cakes and I love music and poetry so we became fast friends. This soft, iced, cake-like cookie was an experiment that he became obsessed with, so now whenever he is performing in London, I make sure they're on his rider.

Makes 12 large cookies

2 (400g) very ripe, soft Hachiya
    persimmons (the acorn-shaped ones)
½ tsp bicarbonate of soda
200g (1 cup) soft light brown sugar
115g (1 stick or ½ cup) unsalted butter
2 tsp vanilla extract
1 egg
300g (2 cups + 2 tbsp) plain flour
½ tsp salt
2 tsp baking powder

For the icing:
80g (¾ stick) unsalted butter
3 tbsp sweetened condensed milk
175g (1½ cups) icing sugar
1 tsp vanilla extract
180g (¾ cup) cream cheese

Baker's tip: Look for large, soft, almost translucent persimmons. In California we call them Hachiya but in England I have never seen this name used – Both the firmer, smaller, more rounded persimmons and these seem to be called Kaki. I find them here in Turkish food shops in the lead up to Christmas.

1. Line 2 baking sheets with baking paper.

2. Use a spoon to scrape out the pulp of the persimmons, removing any seeds. Purée in a food processor or press through a fine sieve. Measure out 300g (1 cup) of persimmon pulp and then combine with the bicarbonate of soda. Set aside to thicken. Reserve the remaining pulp in a sealed container in the fridge until ready to decorate.

3. Cream the sugar and butter together until light and fluffy. Then add the vanilla and eggs and mix until smooth before adding the persimmon pulp mixture, which will have set a little but don't worry.

4. In another bowl, whisk together the flour, salt and baking powder. Add this to the persimmon mixture and beat until smooth. Chill in the fridge for 1 hour. This helps set the butter and thicken the mixture for scooping.

5. Scoop large spoonfuls (or use an ice-cream scoop) onto your prepared baking sheets (you can also bake these in batches if you don't have enough trays or space in your oven).

6. Preheat the oven to 170°C fan/190°C/ 375°F/gas mark 5, then remove the cookies from the fridge and bake for 12–15 minutes until puffed and a slight impression remains when tapped with a finger. Leave to cool completely on the baking tray while you make the icing.

7. Melt the butter in a small saucepan over a medium heat until it starts to sizzle and foam. The white milk solids should settle to the bottom of the pan and start to turn golden brown (if it goes black, you have gone too far and must start again). Swirl the pan a few more times then remove from the heat to cool completely.

8. In the bowl of a stand mixer fitted with the paddle attachment, beat the brown butter, condensed milk, icing sugar and vanilla until smooth. Add the cream cheese and beat just until smooth (do not overbeat or it can become thin).

9. Spread the icing on the cooled cookies. Dollop a teaspoon of the remaining per-simmon pulp over the top of each cookie. These are best eaten on the same day.

CALIFORNIA

BLACKBERRY
and CHILLI PEPPER PIE

Sherry and Tom Baty's ridgetop garden is one of the best suntraps in an otherwise shady Inverness, CA. They grow the best tomatoes, peaches, lemons and some very flavourful red chilli peppers. The story goes that Sherry was making a pie and accidently reached for the cayenne pepper instead of the cinnamon. It was a triumph and she has never gone back. I love these types of kitchen mishaps because we often get stuck thinking something is either in the savoury or sweet category and it takes a mistake to get us to see how delicious new flavour combinations can be.

Serves 8–10

1 quantity of chilled pie dough
    (see page 251)
4 tbsp milk for brushing
4 tbsp caster sugar, for sprinkling

For the filling:
150g caster sugar (¾ cup), plus more
    for sprinkling
4 tbsp cornflour, tapioca or potato starch
Pinch of salt
850g blackberries (4 cups)
1 tbsp lemon juice
Zest of 1 lemon
1 dried red chilli, chopped
85g (¾ stick) unsalted butter, cold and cut
    into 1.5cm (¾in) pieces

Baker's tip: You can also make this pie with frozen blackberries, but if you do, do not let them defrost before baking as they will be too watery.

1. In a clean bowl, whisk together the sugar, cornflour and salt.

2. Tip your blackberries into a large bowl and add the lemon juice and zest and chopped chilli and toss to combine.

3. Preheat the oven to 170°C fan/190°C/ 375°F/gas mark 5.

4. Divide the pastry into two halves, then roll one of them out to a circle big enough to line a 20cm (8in) round pie dish. Spoon in the filling, then dot with the cold butter. Roll out the second half of the pastry and use to create a lattice top: cut the pastry into long strips about 2.5cm (1in) wide. Brush the edges of the pie with a little milk, then lay the strips over the top, weaving them into a lattice design. (See photos on page 252.)

5. Once the pie is assembled, brush the lattice strips with milk and sprinkle with caster sugar. Bake in the oven for 50–60 minutes, until the pastry is golden and the filling is bubbling up out of the lattice top.

GRAPE SLAB PIE

Grape pie is something that caught my eye in a Martha Stewart cookbook published in 1985. This was one of my 'textbooks' and I made every pie in it, at least once. Nothing can compare to the flavour of Concord or Fragola grapes, but they are not as popular because of their astringent skins and large seeds. Although this pie will take you a long time to prepare, it will be so worth it to see the purple smiles of your very satisfied friends.

Serves 12

For the pastry:
560g (4 cups) plain flour, sifted
2 tsp fine sea salt
340g (3 sticks) unsalted butter, chilled
8 tbsp iced water
4 tbsp milk or cream, for brushing
4 tbsp caster sugar, for sprinkling

For the filling:
1.25kg (2lb 11oz) ripe Concord
    or Fragola grapes (weight before
    removing stems)
1 vanilla pod, split lengthways and
    seeds scraped
Zest of 1 lemon
2 tbsp lemon juice
150g (¾ cup) soft light brown sugar
50g (¼ cup) caster sugar
5 tbsp cornflour
½ tsp fine sea salt
A couple of gratings of fresh nutmeg
2 apples, peeled, cored and chopped

1. Whisk together the flour and salt in a large bowl. Add half the butter and cut in, using a round-bladed knife or pastry cutter. Combine well using a cutting motion. Add the remaining butter and continue to mix until you have roughly pea-sized pieces.

2. Sprinkle over the iced water (holding back the ice) and toss it through the mix as you go. The dough should start to become raggedy and eventually, when all the water is added, it will come together into a ball. Divide the ball in half, wrapping each piece in clingfilm. Pat them into flat squares and rest in the fridge for at least 20 minutes or up to 24 hours. (Any longer than this, put it in the freezer.)

3. To make the filling, strip the grapes off the stems, then separate the skins from the pulp by pinching each grape to squeeze out the pulp into a heavy-based saucepan. Set the skins aside. Add the scraped vanilla pod and seeds, plus the lemon zest and heat gently until the pulp is soft and beginning to separate from the grape seeds, about 10 minutes.

4. Pour the pulp through a mesh sieve placed over a bowl. Press through with a plastic pastry scraper or the back of a wooden spoon until all the pulp is in the bowl. Discard the grape seeds. Rinse and dry out the vanilla pod for another purpose. Add the lemon juice to the pulp.

5. In another large bowl, whisk together the sugars, cornflour, salt and nutmeg. Slowly whisk the strained grape mixture into the sugar mixture and add the grape skins back in. Add the apples to the grape mixture.

CALIFORNIA

6. Butter and flour a baking tray that measures 23×33cm (9×13in) and has a lip about 2.5cm (1in) deep.

7. Roll out one square of pastry on a lightly floured surface to roughly 28×38cm (11×15in). Press the pastry down into the prepared baking tray, then chill in the fridge while you roll out the other piece. The second pastry sheet (which will form the top of the pie) can be rolled out to 23×33cm (9×13in). Remove the pastry-lined baking tray from the fridge and carefully fill it with the grape mixture. It can come right up to about 2mm shy of the top of the tin but don't let it overflow. Roll the top layer of pastry over the pie. Brush the pastry with milk. Fold or roll over the excess pastry and pinch to seal. Use a knife to pierce the top of the pie a few times. Put in your freezer or fridge for 20 minutes.

8. Preheat the oven to 180°C fan/200°C/ 400°F/gas mark 6.

9. Brush the edge and top of the pie with the milk or cream and sprinkle over the caster sugar. Line the bottom of your oven with foil to catch any drips, then bake the pie for about 25 minutes. Reduce the heat to 160°C fan/180°C/350°F/gas mark 4 and bake for another 35–45 minutes, or until golden and the filling is bubbling up through the pastry. Cool for 3 hours before slicing.

PINK APPLE, LIME
and BEE POLLEN GALETTE

Pink apples are not easily found in supermarkets but can be found at some farmer's markets. Every child I know loves them and frankly so do most adults. But any tart, crisp apple will do in this recipe – and the addition of a few raspberries will give a hint of pink to your tart.

Serves 6–8

½ quantity of chilled wholemeal galette pastry (see page 258)
8 medium pink-fleshed apples
1 tbsp bee pollen, crushed in a mortar and pestle
Zest and juice of 1 lime
2 tbsp butter, melted
80g (¼ cup + 2 tbsp) caster sugar
Handful of raspberries
Cream or ice cream, to serve

For the glaze/sauce:
Apple peelings and cores from above apples
500g apple juice (2 cups)
100g (½ cup) caster sugar

1. Remove the pastry from the fridge and let it soften slightly while you prepare the apples.

2. Peel, quarter and core your apples. Save all the peels and cores, put them into a small saucepan and set aside. Slice each quarter into 3mm (⅛ in) slices. Take all of the small end pieces of apple and coarsely chop them up with a few of the nice slices to make about a handful of chopped apple. Set this aside. Don't worry about the apples browning because this will disappear once they are baked.

3. Line a heavy baking sheet or pizza pan with baking paper. Roll out the pastry into a large circle about 30cm (12in) in diameter, then slide the pastry onto the paper-lined baking sheet. Make a border of apple slices around the perimeter of the pastry, about 4cm (1½in) from the edge. Sprinkle the chopped apples in a thin layer inside the ring of apple slices and sprinkle with the crushed bee pollen and lime zest and juice. Arrange the apple slices in a pretty pattern so that they are overlapping and you don't see any of the pastry or chopped apples poking through underneath. Add your raspberries on top. Roll the pastry up over the border of apples tightly and place in the fridge to chill while you preheat the oven to 180°C fan/200°C/400°F/gas mark 6.

4. Remove the galette from the fridge and brush the pastry edge with the melted butter. Sprinkle about half the caster sugar over the apples and the other half over the pastry edge (this will give it a nice crunch once baked). Place the galette in the oven and bake for 45–60 minutes.

5. While the galette bakes you can prepare the sauce. Add the apple juice and sugar to the pan of peels and cores and place over a medium heat for 20 minutes, stirring occasionally. Strain the sauce and put it back in the pan to reduce the liquid for another 10 minutes.

6. When the galette is golden and bubbly, remove the baking sheet from the oven and place on a wire rack for 10 minutes to rest. Slide the galette, still on the baking paper, off the baking sheet and onto the wire rack to cool for another 10 minutes. Finally remove the paper and cool further. (These steps are to achieve a crisp pastry that isn't soggy.) Serve warm or at room temperature, with the apple sauce and cream or ice cream.

PEACH, NECTARINE and LARD PIE

This deep-dish open-face pie is adapted from a method taught to me by the wonderful chef of American Southern cuisine, Scott Peacock, who learned it from the award-winning chef, his dear friend Edna Lewis. Miss Lewis was the granddaughter of formerly enslaved people and made the case for Black Southern cooking as the foundation of American cuisine. Scott and I made these pie-cobblers together for the 40th anniversary of Chez Panisse at a shrimp boil at Alice Water's house in Berkeley.

Serves 6–8

1 quantity of lard pastry (see page 257)
2 tbsp cream, for brushing
2 tbsp caster sugar, for sprinkling
Cream, to serve

For the peach filling:
1kg (2lb 4oz) peaches and nectarines
200g (1 cup) caster sugar
1 tbsp cornflour
2 tsp vanilla extract
¼ tsp almond extract
80g (¾ stick) unsalted butter
Pinch of salt

Baker's tip: The use of lard in the pasty is what makes it so flaky while keeping a crisp bottom. The butter is there for flavour. If I were not catering to different dietary requests, I would choose this pastry every time for pies, no question.

1. Butter a 23cm (9in) pie dish or gratin dish.

2. Roll the pastry out into a 23×18cm (9×7in) oblong dish. Place inside your prepared dish so that the edges hang well over the sides. Set aside in the fridge while you make the filling.

3. Cut each peach and nectarine into eighths, removing the stones. Whisk together the sugar, cornflour and salt and toss well with the peaches. Add the vanilla and almond extracts and toss again.

4. Preheat the oven to 180°C fan/200°C/ 400°F/gas mark 6.

5. Remove the pastry-lined dish from the fridge and fill with the peaches and nectarines and dot with the butter. Fold the pastry overhang roughly over the fruit, pinching the corners. Brush the pastry edges with cream and sprinkle with sugar.

6. Bake for 45–50 minutes, or until the pastry is golden and the fruit is bubbling. Leave to cool for at least 2 hours before serving, with cream on the side.

PISTACHIO GREEN PLUM CAKE with CANDIED VIOLETS

This cake is all about colour. Whether using greengages, emerald plums, or green or yellow pluots, the pale plums look gorgeous alongside the yellow-green pistachios. The candied violets add a little colour but also a subtle floral note which I love. This is a great cake to have with tea in the afternoon but I would also make this cake for breakfast if I'm honest!

Serves 6–8

175g (1½ sticks) unsalted butter
200g (1 cup) caster sugar, plus more
    for sprinkling
2 eggs
150g (1 cup) pistachios, very
    finely chopped
140g (1 cup) plain flour
2 tsp baking powder
½ tsp fine sea salt
400g (14oz) green plums or pluots, halved
Candied violets, to finish
Greek yoghurt, to serve

1. Preheat the oven to 160°C fan/180°C/ 350°F/gas mark 4. Grease and line a 20×15cm (8×6in) cake tin with baking paper.

2. In the bowl of a stand mixer fitted with the paddle attachment, cream the butter and sugar until very pale and fluffy. Scrape down the sides and slowly beat in the eggs one at a time. Add the chopped pistachios to the mix and combine well.

3. In a separate bowl, whisk together the flour, baking powder and salt. Add this to the cake mixture and mix until just combined.

4. Spread the mixture into your prepared tin, then press the plums cut-side up into the batter so that there is a fairly even covering of plums.

5. Sprinkle a little extra caster sugar over the top of the plums, scatter some of the candied violets, reserving some for after baking, and bake for 40–45 minutes, or until the top of the cake is golden and a skewer inserted into the centre comes out clean.

6. Serve warm or room temperature with thick Greek yoghurt, sprinkled with more candied violets.

WILD FENNEL
and ROASTED FIG
FRIANDS

All along the highways and boulevards of Northern California in the late summer and early autumn, you will see shoulder-high wild fennel plants blooming yellow and silhouetting your drive. Roll down the window and the warming scent is unmistakable. My father Gene foraged the wild fennel used for this book near our family home, but I see it growing in London in the autumn too. Friands are little French almond cakes that are moist and nutty and a perfect vehicle for roasted seasonal fruits.

Makes 24 friands

For the roasted figs
10 ripe black figs
150g (5½oz) raspberries
120g (½ cup) Muscat wine
50g (¼ cup) caster sugar
2 fronds of wild or cultivated fennel leaves
Honey, for drizzling
2–4 wild fennel heads full of yellow pollen

For the friands
115g (1 stick or ½ cup) unsalted butter
90g (⅘ cup) plain flour
¾ tsp baking powder
50g (½ cup) ground almonds
80g (⅘ cup) ground hazelnuts
190g (1½ cups) icing sugar
5 egg whites, slightly whisked
2 tsp vanilla extract
25g (1oz) hazelnuts, sliced in half

Baker's tip: If you can't find wild fennel, crush some fennel seeds with a pestle and mortar and use that in place of the pollen.

1. Preheat the oven to 180°C fan/200°C/400°F/gas mark 6. Select a ceramic or other heavy roasting dish that will hold the figs snugly – about 20cm (8in) in diameter.

2. Trim the tough tip of the stem on each fig but try to maintain the lovely fig shape. Cut the figs into quarters through the tail and stem, then put in your baking dish, cut side facing up. Scatter with the raspberries and pour over the Muscat wine. Sprinkle evenly with caster sugar and gently lay the fennel fronds over the top. Bake for about 30 minutes, or until the figs have puffed up and the wine has reduced a little. Remove from the oven and allow to cool for 10 minutes.

3. While the figs are still warm, drizzle with honey and sprinkle over the pollen from the heads of fennel by gently pulling the flowers. Do this over the figs to catch all the falling goodness. Set aside while you prepare the friand batter.

4. Reduce the oven temperature to 160°C fan/180°C/350°F/gas mark 4 and grease 24 friand moulds or mini cupcake tins thoroughly.

5. In a small saucepan over a medium heat, melt the butter until it starts to sizzle and foam. The white milk solids should settle to the bottom of the pan and start to turn golden brown (if it goes black, you have gone too far and must start again). Swirl the pan a few more times then remove from the heat to cool slightly.

6. Add all the remaining ingredients, except the halved hazelnuts, to the bowl of a food processor. Add the cooled browned butter and blitz until foamy, about 1 minute.

7. Spoon the mixture into the moulds, filling them to about three-quarters full, then top each friand with a piece or two of roasted fig and a roasted raspberry. Add a half hazelnut, cut-side up and drizzle with a ¼ teaspoon of the fig roasting liquid.

8. Bake for about 15–20 minutes until the tops of the cakes are springy to the touch.

9. Leave the cakes to cool slightly in their moulds; don't leave them for more than 10 minutes as the fig liquid can become too sticky, making them hard to unmould. Pop them out and sprinkle with a little more fennel pollen. If they do get stuck in the tins, pop them back into the oven for a few minutes and then they should come right out. They will keep well in an airtight container for a few days.

LEMON MERINGUE
PIE BARS

This recipe originally came from my mom, Elisabeth. She always made excellent lemon bars when I was growing up. Mom loves anything lemony and tart and I'm just the same. I'm so lucky that she is always so willing to share her recipes with me. We make these at the bakery with a torched meringue topping for fun. It's worth getting a small kitchen blowtorch to raise the bar of presentation in your home baking.

Makes 9–12

For the shortbread base:
255g (1¾ cups) plain flour
80g (½ cup + 2 tbsp) icing sugar
½ tsp salt
200g (¾ cup + 2 tbsp) unsalted butter, cold, cut into cubes

For the lemon filling:
55g (¼ cup + 2 tbsp) plain flour
1½ tsp baking powder
500g (2½ cups) caster sugar
4 eggs
3–4 lemons, zested and juiced (you need about 175g/¾ cup lemon juice)

For the meringue topping:
4 egg whites
200g (1 cup) caster sugar
2 tbsp golden syrup
Pinch of salt
2 tbsp vanilla extract

Baker's tip: You will need a piping bag and nozzle to get the shell effect, or you can simply make a nice swoopy pattern with a palette knife or butter knife like a traditional lemon meringue pie.

1. Preheat the oven to 170°C fan/190°C/ 375°F/gas mark 5 and grease and line a 20×30cm (8×12in) baking tray with baking paper. Do not cut the corners of the paper to fit the tray, just line as tightly as possible so that the paper comes above the edge of the tray on all sides.

2. Put the flour, icing sugar and salt into a food processor and pulse briefly to combine, then add the cubed butter and pulse until it comes together in a ball.

3. Press the mixture evenly into the prepared baking tray, then bake for 20–25 minutes until golden.

4. Meanwhile, prepare the filling. Put the flour, baking powder and caster sugar into a large bowl and use a hand-held electric whisk to combine. Add the eggs and lemon juice and whisk again. Strain the mixture into a clean bowl and stir in the lemon zest.

5. As soon as the base is baked, remove from the oven, carefully pour over the topping and return to the oven. Immediately lower the temperature to 160°C fan/180°C/350°F/ gas mark 4 and bake for about 30 minutes, or until the top is set; it should be slightly firm and golden. Remove from the oven and allow to cool completely.

6. Meanwhile, put all the ingredients for the meringue topping into a heatproof bowl and place over a saucepan of boiling water (do not let the water touch the bottom of the bowl or it will cook the egg whites). Whisk continuously until the sugar dissolves and the mixture is very warm to the touch. If using a sugar thermometer, whisk continuously for 2 minutes, or until it reads 70–75°C (158–167°F) – whichever comes first. Transfer to the

bowl of a stand mixer fitted with a whisk attachment (or use a hand-held electric whisk) to whip the mixture into stiff, glossy peaks.

7. Put the marshmallow into a piping bag fitted with your favourite nozzle (I like to use a Wilton 6B, 2B or 1M). Pipe (or spoon) the meringue onto the cooled lemon filling. You can either cover the entire tray or slice into 12 bars first and then pipe each one individually, as we do at the bakery.

8. If you have a blowtorch, torch the top of the meringue, or if you're brave you can pop it under the grill for 30 seconds or so to get the same effect.

9. These are best enjoyed on the same day but will keep at room temperature for 24 hours.

GREY SALT, WHITE CHOCOLATE MATCHA BLONDIES

I used to turn my nose up at white chocolate, but thank goodness I'm over that. It has that gorgeous melt that only comes from chocolate but the flavour is rich and creamy, often with hints of vanilla. The bitter green flavour of matcha is slightly muted by the grey salt which I use here for the colour as well as the coarse texture.

Makes 12 blondies

250g (1 cup + 2 tbsp) unsalted butter
2 eggs
300g (1½ cups) caster sugar
2 tbsp vanilla extract
240g (1¾ cups) plain flour
1 tbsp matcha powder
1½ tsp baking powder
1½ tsp sea salt
200g (7oz) white chocolate, chopped
¼ tsp grey salt, for sprinkling

1. Preheat the oven to 140°C fan/160°C/325°F/gas mark 3. Grease and line a 30×20cm (12×8in) cake tin with baking paper.

2. Gently melt butter in a small pan and set aside to cool slightly. In a large bowl, whisk together eggs, sugar and vanilla until frothy, then whisk in the melted butter.

3. Whisk together the flour, matcha powder, baking powder and salt before adding to the wet ingredients along with the white chocolate pieces. Mix until just combined.

4. Pour the mixture into your prepared tin and smooth the top, then sprinkle with the grey salt and bake in the oven for 30 minutes. The centre should be puffed and set but still a little gooey.

AFTER a MEAL

PEACHES and CREAM
ANGEL FOOD CAKE

In England, I never see angel food cake, and it's a shame because it's a fine cake. Light and spongy, it's the perfect vehicle for seasonal fruit and perfectly whipped cream. My favourite way to serve it is with peeled ripe white peaches.

Serves 6–8

4 tbsp cornflour
140g (1 cup) plain flour
190g (1½ cups) icing sugar
12 egg whites
1½ tsp cream of tartar
¼ tsp salt
1½ tsp vanilla extract
½ tsp almond extract
200g (1 cup) caster sugar
2 ripe white peaches
360g (1½ cups) double cream

1. Preheat the oven to 170°C fan/190°C/ 375°F/gas mark 5. Have ready a sparkling clean, ungreased angel food cake tin 25cm (10in) in diameter and 10cm (4in) deep. The reason we don't grease the tin is to make the cake stick to the sides of the tin. This will allow the cake to be tall and lighter than air.

2. Sift the cornflour, flour and icing sugar into a large bowl and set aside.

3. Add the egg whites, cream of tartar, salt and vanilla and almond extracts to the bowl of a stand mixer fitted with the whisk attachment. Start whisking on medium speed, gradually adding the sugar a couple of tablespoons at a time. Continue until you have stiff, glossy peaks.

4. Gradually fold in the dry ingredients, being careful not to knock out too much air.

5. Gently spoon the mixture into the tin. Cut through the batter with a knife to remove air pockets. Bake until lightly browned and the entire top appears dry, 35–40 minutes. Immediately invert the tin and allow the cake to cool completely, about 1 hour, before removing the cake from the tin.

6. While the cake is cooling, blanch the peaches. Bring a large saucepan of water to the boil. Have ready a large bowl of iced water and a slotted spoon or small sieve to fish out the blanched peaches. Gently lower the peaches into the boiling water (don't overcrowd the pan). The peaches will only need about 30 seconds in the water to loosen the skins. Lift one up out of the water and pinch the skin to see if it is ready to slide off. If the skin is still clinging to the flesh of the peach, slip it back into the water for a few more seconds. If it's peelable, gently add it to the bowl of iced water. Continue until all the peaches have been blanched. Set aside in the iced water until ready to serve.

7. When ready to serve with the cake, use a thin-bladed knife to loosen the cake from the edges of the tin and the centre ring. Pop the cake out onto a serving plate. Whip the cream to soft peaks, slip the skins off the peaches, quarter and slice them to remove the stones and serve with a slice of cake.

CALIFORNIA

BASQUE CHEESECAKE

There has been a real trend for this cake in the last few years, and for good reason. Some are small and perfectly formed, some are rustic and family-style. They hail from the Basque region of Spain, but one of the best ones I've tried is from Brat Restaurant in London where everything is cooked in the fire and where I go far more often than I should admit. But what I love about this cake is that it has no base or pastry. Just cheese, cream and some sugar cooked at a high heat to get a scorched exterior with a creamy, wobbly interior.

Serves 6

450g (1¾ cups) cream cheese
125g (½ cup + 2 tbsp) sugar
3 eggs
250g (1 cup) double cream
1 tbsp crème fraîche
1 tbsp vanilla extract
1 tbsp tapioca flour
1 tbsp cornflour
¼ tsp sea salt

1. Preheat the oven to 230°C fan/250°C/475°F/gas mark 9. Line a 15cm (6in) round cake tin that it is at least 8cm (3in) deep with a single sheet of baking paper that comes all the way up the sides and out of the tin. This cake rises up, then sinks back down, so the extra paper is crucial.

2. In the bowl of a stand mixer fitted with the paddle attachment (or by hand with a balloon whisk), whip together the cream cheese and sugar until smooth. Add the eggs one at a time, whisking after each addition.

3. In a separate bowl whisk together the remaining ingredients until smooth, then add to the cheese mixture and mix until smooth and combined.

4. Pour the mixture into the prepared tin and bake in the oven for 40 minutes until it's black on top and puffed but still has a little wobble. Cool for at least 1 hour until set. Serve at room temperature.

This cake is inspired by my favourite cake at The River Café. My friend Ruthie Rogers (the restaurant's co-founder) always makes each guest feel like the most important person in the room. When I first moved to London, I tried to get a job at her restaurant but at the time they didn't have a pastry team, so I ended up answering phones. When the other co-founder, Rose Gray, saw me she asked what the hell I was doing there – not only I was terrible at phones, but I belonged in the kitchen. Now, 18 years later, they have a full pastry team, and I tease Ruthie that I should apply for a job.

Serves 8

250g (1¼ cups) whole hazelnuts, skins on
250g (9oz) dark chocolate
250g (2 sticks + 2 tbsp) unsalted butter
6 eggs, at room temperature
½ tsp fine sea salt
250g (1¼ cups) caster sugar
¼ tsp flaky sea salt for top
Crème fraîche or whipped cream,
    to serve

1. Preheat the oven to 150°C fan/170°C/ 340°F/gas mark 3½ and grease and line a 20cm (8in) cake tin with baking paper.

2. I recommend using whole hazelnuts with the skins on and going through the process of toasting and removing the skins yourself. You can buy toasted blanched hazelnuts but the flavour is inferior as they deteriorate much quicker once toasted and so inevitably taste slightly stale. Toast the hazelnuts on a baking tray until deep golden and the skins are cracking off, about 15 minutes. (Watch they don't burn as this will spoil the flavour of the cake.) Remove the nuts from the oven and turn them out onto a clean tea towel. Bring up the sides of the towel to make a little satchel and rub the nuts together to slough off the skins as much as possible. Open the cloth up and carefully lift out the toasted nuts, leaving behind as much of the skins as possible. Place the skinned toasted nuts into a food processor and blitz until roughly chopped but not a powder. Set aside.

3. In a heatproof bowl set over a pot of simmering water (make sure the bottom of the bowl is not touching the water) melt the chocolate and butter, stirring occasionally. Once melted remove from the heat and allow to cool slightly, but keep away from draughts.

4. Meanwhile in the bowl of a stand mixer fitted with the whisk attachment, whip up the eggs and fine sea salt until frothy, then slowly add the sugar in a couple of batches. Whip until fluffy and voluminous.

5. Stir the chopped hazelnuts into the melted chocolate and butter mixture. Finally fold in the whipped eggs and sugar. Pour into the prepared cake tin and sprinkle the top with the flaky sea salt. Bake for 30 minutes until set but not dry. You want the centre to be a little wobbly and gooey; it will continue to bake and set as it cools, so don't look for a clean skewer test here. Cool for at least an hour before cutting and serving with the crème fraîche or softly whipped cream.

CALIFORNIA

LATE SUMMER PEACH TARTE TATIN with PEACH LEAF CUSTARD

Oren is a great little restaurant around the corner from my flat in Hackney. It's Mediterranean-inspired, simple, delicious fare. It's the type of place you want to visit once a week. The Israeli-born chef-owner Oded is a good baker. His loaves of challah and perfect pillows of pitta bread accompany the food while the desserts are seasonal classics. One of my favourites is a peach tarte tatin. Since trying his, I prefer using peaches to the typical apples. I serve mine with a light custard steeped with fresh peach leaves, which taste of green almonds.

Serves 8–10

For the custard:
3 egg yolks
480g (2 cups) single cream
2 tbsp caster sugar
30–40 peach leaves, washed and dried
    (If you can't get the leaves, add a
    drop or two of almond extract to the
    custard instead)
Pinch of salt

For the tarte:
8–10 large ripe but firm peaches
3 tbsp unsalted butter
135g (½ cup + 3 tbsp) caster sugar
500g (1lb 2oz) puff pastry (see page 253),
    rolled into a 30cm (12in) circle
    and chilled

Baker's tip: The final step is quite fun to do at the table, so I love to get the custard made and the tart all prepped up to the last stage of tucking in the pastry, then chilling in the fridge until you sit down to dinner. Then you can pop it into the oven while you eat. This way you can flip it out onto a serving plate right in front of your guests.

1. Make the custard. Separate your egg yolks into a small bowl, reserving the egg whites for another use (they freeze well!). Add the single cream and sugar to a heavy-based saucepan and place over a medium heat until foaming and hot but not boiling. Take a handful of peach leaves and steep them in the steaming cream for about 30 seconds. Dunk them and stir them around as they steep, then remove and discard the used leaves before adding another fresh handful. Repeat until all leaves have been used and the cream is a pale shade of green. To achieve the bright, fresh, peach-leaf flavour, you must work swiftly. Leaving the leaves for too long in the custard changes the flavour and is undesirable. Next, temper the egg yolks with a few tablespoons of the warm cream, whisking until smooth. Add the tempered yolks back into the remaining cream, moving a heatproof spatula or wooden spoon along the bottom of the pan continuously. As soon as the custard thickens on the bottom of the pan, turn off the heat, stir in the salt and pour the custard through a strainer and into a jug. Chill completely in the fridge.

2. Next, blanch the peaches. Bring a large saucepan of water to the boil. Have ready a large bowl of iced water and have a slotted spoon or small sieve to fish out the blanched peaches. Gently lower the peaches into the boiling water (don't overcrowd the pan). The peaches will only need about 30 seconds in the water to loosen the skins. Lift one up out of the water and pinch the skin to see if it is ready to slide off. If the skin is still clinging to the flesh of the peach, slip it back into the water for a few more seconds. If it's peelable, gently add it to the bowl of iced water. Continue until all the peaches have been blanched, then lift them out of the water bath and slip off the skins. Cut the peaches in half, remove the stones and cut into quarters. Set aside on a plate. Don't worry about any oxidisation that occurs as this will disappear when baked.

3. Preheat the oven to 200°C fan/220°C/ 425°F/gas mark 7. Prepare a bowl of iced water large enough for a 25cm (10in) cast-iron frying pan or copper tatin mould (or you could set this up in your kitchen sink).

4. Caramelise 2 tablespoons of the butter and 6 tablespoons of the sugar over a high heat, swirling the pan now and then. Once the sugar has dissolved, use

AFTER a MEAL

a wooden spoon or balloon whisk to bring it all together. Do not worry if it splits or crystallises, as it will dissolve again during the baking process. You want a deep, dark caramel. Remove from the heat and immediately put the pan in the iced water to stop the caramel from colouring any further.

5. Arrange the peaches in the pan of caramel, bearing in mind they will be upside down when done, so make them look pretty. I place the curved side down into the caramel, core side up. Place a second layer of peaches on top, core side down, and press gently with your hands, coaxing them to fit together like a puzzle.

6. Cover with the chilled pastry circle, tucking the edges in between the peaches and the pan, then melt the remaining tablespoon of butter and brush the pastry with it. Sprinkle with the remaining 3 tablespoons sugar, then pierce several times with a knife to allow steam to escape during baking.

7. Bake the tarte tatin for 45–55 minutes, or until the pastry is crisp and golden, the sugar has started to caramelise on top, and the peaches and caramel beneath are starting to bubble up at the edges.

8. Remove the tarte from the oven and allow to sit undisturbed for 10 minutes. Have ready a large plate that will completely cover the top of the tarte tatin. Using extreme caution, place the plate over the pan and, using an oven glove or tea towel wrapped around the outside, quickly flip the pan over and turn the tart out onto the plate in one smooth motion, being cautious of any hot liquid or steam that might escape. Serve with cold peach leaf custard.

AFTER a MEAL

POACHED PEAR
PAVLOVA

The combination of textures and the alternating from sweet to rich to boozy in every bite is unparalleled in other puddings. While I have been making a version of this recipe for years, it was having pavlova at chef Jeremy Lee's Quo Vadis in Soho, London that solidified my love. There's something about his perfect palate, extraordinary hospitality, way with storytelling and Scottish accent that all combine to make his desserts the best in London.

Serves 6

For the meringues:
3 egg whites
¼ tsp salt
½ tsp white vinegar
1 tsp vanilla extract
250g (1¼ cups) caster sugar
1½ tsp cornflour

For the poached pears:
750g (3 cups) Muscat wine
360g (1½ cups) water
300g (1½ cups) caster sugar
Zest and juice of 1 lemon
1 star anise
3 large pears

To serve:
Crème fraîche
Vanilla ice cream
Honey, for drizzling
Reduced poaching liquid
Honeysuckle flowers, to decorate
    (optional)

1. Preheat the oven to 100°C fan/120°C/ 250°F/gas mark ½ and line a baking sheet with baking paper.

2. Using a handheld electric whisk, beat the egg whites, salt, vinegar and vanilla together on a high speed until soft peaks form.

3. Whisk the sugar and cornflour together in a separate bowl, then add half to the frothy egg whites. Whisk until very stiff and then add the remaining sugar mixture and whisk again until smooth and glossy.

4. Spoon 6 portions of meringue onto the prepared baking sheet using two tablespoons and spacing them about 4cm (1½ in) apart. Make a hollow in the centre of each one with the back of the spoon. Bake for about 2 hours. Remove from the oven and immediately transfer the meringues off the baking tray and onto a cooling rack to cool completely.

5. While the meringues are baking, poach the pears. In a heavy-based saucepan that is just large enough to hold 3 pears, add all the ingredients except the pears. Heat slowly to dissolve the sugar.

6. Peel the pears whole, keeping the stem intact if possible, and gently lower them into the poaching liquid. Cook at a slow simmer (bubbles no larger than champagne) for 45 minutes–1 hour – they should be soft when pierced with the tip of a knife.

7. Carefully lift the pears from the poaching liquid with a slotted spoon and place onto a plate or dish to cool. When cool, cut each pear in half and carefully remove the cores.

8. Put the pan back over a high heat and reduce the poaching liquid by half.

9. When you are ready to serve, place a meringue onto each plate with a dollop of crème fraîche. Place half a poached pear on top then top with ice cream, drizzled honey, more creme fraîche and a spoonful of the reduced poaching liquid. If you have honeysuckle growing you could scatter with a few of the flowers too.

STICKY TOFFEE DATE PUDDING

This is a very British recipe, but I always associate dates with California, so it's one of those recipes that bridges the two cultures perfectly. The English way of making toffee caramelises the cream with the sugar. I was taught to caramelise the sugar alone, then stop the cooking process with cold cream, but this English style gives a unique almost fudgy flavour that really goes well with the dates. This recipe would be amazing made with unpasteurised goat's milk, which gives an earthy tang. Do give it a try if you can get some.

Serves 6–8

250g (9oz) pitted dates
240g (1 cup) boiling water
1 tsp bicarbonate of soda
85g (¾ stick) unsalted butter
2 eggs
200g (1 cup) dark brown sugar
2 tsp vanilla extract
140g (1 cup) plain flour
1 tsp baking powder
½ tsp sea salt
Crème fraîche, to serve

For the sauce:
480g (2 cups) double cream
230g (1 cup + 2 tbsp) caster sugar
1 vanilla pod, split lengthways
55g (½ stick) chilled unsalted butter, cut into pieces
Fleur de sel (which has the best texture for caramel but any good sea salt will do)

1. Preheat the oven to 160°C fan/180°C/350°F/gas mark 4. Lightly butter a small baking dish, about 20×15×8cm (8×6×3in).

2. Put the dates into a heatproof bowl and pour over the boiling water and the bicarbonate of soda. Give them a stir and let them sit until soft and almost all the water has been absorbed, about 15 minutes. Drain the dates and tip into a food processor, then blitz to a smooth paste. Set aside to cool.

3. Melt the butter in a small saucepan over a low heat and set aside to cool.

4. In a large bowl, whisk together the eggs, sugar and vanilla extract until pale and frothy. Set aside.

5. In another bowl (sorry, so many bowls!) whisk together the flour, baking powder and salt. Set aside.

6. Stir the date paste and cooled melted butter into the frothy egg mixture until well combined, then stir in the flour mixture. Transfer to your prepared baking dish and bake for 45 minutes, or until set.

7. While the cake is baking, prepare the sauce. Put half of the cream into a heavy-based saucepan and add the sugar. Scrape the seeds from the vanilla pod and add them in with the scraped pod. Place over a medium heat, stirring constantly until caramelised and reduced. Take off the heat, remove the vanilla pod and whisk in the chilled butter, a few pieces at a time, until melted. Add the remaining cream and fleur de sel.

8. Cut slices of the date pudding and serve warm with sauce poured on top and a dollop of crème fraîche on the side.

TRIPLE CREAM
AMARETTO CHEESECAKE

I love the amaretti cookies you find in Italian delis. I remember when I was a child watching a man in a café make a mini hot air balloon out of one of their beautiful paper wrappers. It literally went up in flames before gently extinguishing and floating back down to the table. This cheesecake is a perfect excuse to use these nostalgic bitter almond cookies. The three creams are because... well, why not? Oh and that whole thing about baking cheesecakes in messy water baths? Forget it. This technique works well and you will never get a soggy bottom again.

Serves 6–8

For the base:
200g (7oz) amaretti cookies, crushed
50g (½ cup) ground almonds
115g (1 stick) unsalted butter
⅛ tsp fine sea salt

For the filling:
690g (1½lb) cream cheese
100g (½ cup) soft light brown sugar
4 eggs
1 tsp vanilla extract
250g (1 cup) crème fraîche
120g (½ cup) double cream
3 tbsp amaretto

1. Grease a 23cm (9in) springform cake tin.

2. Crush the amaretti cookies into a bowl by hand and add the ground almonds. Melt the butter in a small saucepan, then add to the bowl, along with the salt, and combine well with a spoon. Press into the bottom of your prepared baking tin and chill for at least 30 minutes while you make the filling.

3. In the bowl of a stand mixer, cream together the cream cheese and sugar, then add the eggs one at a time, mixing thoroughly after each addition. Add the crème fraîche, cream and amaretto and mix again until well combined.

4. Preheat the oven to 150°C fan/170°C/ 340°F/gas mark 3½.

5. Remove the base from the fridge and top the crust with the cheese mixture, smoothing the top. Your cake tin will be very full, but don't worry. Place on a baking sheet and into the middle of the oven. Bake for 1 hour until golden and set around the edges, but still wobbly in the middle.

6. Turn the oven off and prop the door open with a wooden spoon. Leave the cheesecake inside to cool for at least an hour then place in the fridge and chill until ready to serve.

AFTER a MEAL

PEAR EVE'S PUDDING

An old-fashioned English dessert, Eve's pudding is usually made with apples (hence the biblical name). This fluffy sponge topping works well with any fruit you might put into a cobbler, crumble or crisp, so I put it into the California section of the book, where we make those a lot. We photographed this book during pear season, so we use them here to great effect. I love the subtle fragrance of pears which often gets lost under cinnamon and other spices. This plain sponge is perfect for them.

Serves 6–8

6–8 ripe Warren or Comice pears
4 tbsp soft light brown sugar
Zest and juice of 1 lemon
2 tbsp caster sugar, for sprinkling
Cream, to serve

For the topping:
250g (2 sticks + 2 tbsp) unsalted butter
250g (1¼ cups) caster sugar
2 eggs
250g (1¾ cups) plain flour
2 tsp baking powder
¼ tsp salt
80g (⅓ cup) milk

1. Preheat the oven to 160°C fan/180°C/ 350°F/gas mark 4 and butter a large, oval baking dish.

2. Peel and core the pears, then chop into 2cm (¾in) pieces. Put these into a saucepan with the brown sugar and lemon zest and juice.

3. Cook over a low-medium heat for 5–10 minutes to soften the pears, then turn them into the prepared dish and set aside while you make the topping.

4. Cream the butter and sugar until pale and fluffy, then add the eggs, one at a time. Add the flour, baking powder and salt and mix well, then stir in the milk, until just combined (avoid overmixing at this point).

5. Spoon the topping over the pears, sprinkle with the caster sugar and bake for 35–40 minutes, or until golden and springy to the touch. Serve warm with plenty of cold unwhipped cream.

AFTER a MEAL

CALIFORNIA

PARTY PARTY

STACKED
BLACKBERRY JAM CAKE

Delicious and light, this cake is perfect for a late summer outdoor meal. It is made using the reverse creaming method, which adds the fat to the dry ingredients first rather than creaming the butter with the sugar. This method produces a fluffy and moist texture that I love. The egg whites make the sponge bright white which looks striking against the purple-black jam. Decorate with coconut for a retro look or berries and flowers for a garden party – or both!

For the jam:
300g (10½oz) blackberries
   (or raspberries or loganberries)
250g (1¼ cups) granulated sugar
4 geranium leaves or 8 verbena leaves

For the cake:
350g (2½ cups) plain flour
1 tbsp baking powder
½ tsp sea salt
300g (1½ cups) caster sugar
190g (¾ cup + 2 tbsp) unsalted butter,
   very soft
5 egg whites
240g (1 cup) whole milk
1 tbsp vanilla extract

1. Reserve a small handful of blackberries for decoration, placing them in the freezer. Put the remaining berries into a medium non-reactive heavy-bottomed saucepan, to avoid burning. Cover with half of the sugar and add the torn geranium or verbena leaves. Set aside to macerate.

2. Grease and line a baking tray that is 2.5cm (1in) deep, and roughly 23×33cm (9×13in). Preheat the oven to 160°C fan/ 180°C/350°F/gas mark 4.

3. Add the flour, baking powder, salt and sugar to the bowl of a stand mixer fitted with the paddle attachment. Beat well to combine, then add the soft butter and mix again until a sandy texture forms.

4. In a jug whisk together the egg whites, milk and vanilla. Turn the mixer down to a low speed and with the mixer running, add the wet ingredients in a steady stream. Once added, turn the speed to high and beat until light and fluffy.

5. Pour the mixture into the prepared tin, then bake for 30–40 minutes, or until golden and springs back to the touch.

6. Meanwhile, finish the jam. Line a small roasting tray with baking paper and tip the remaining sugar onto it. Place in the oven to warm for about 10 minutes.

7. Heat the macerated berries until just warm and gently mash with a fruit or potato masher or something similar. Add the warmed sugar and stir until the sugar dissolves, then bring to the boil and cook for 15 minutes, stirring periodically. Allow to cool completely.

8. Remove the cake from the oven and leave it to cool in the tin. Once the cake has cooled, remove it from the tin and cut into 4, using a ruler to get perfectly. Stack the 4 quarters together and using a long serrated knife (bread knife) trim the edges neatly and evenly. Unstack them again, placing one layer onto a serving platter. Spread with a thin layer of jam. Repeat with the remaining layers. Sprinkle with the reserved frozen berries, coconut or flowers and serve.

9. Store any unused jam in the fridge in jars or a container with a tight-fitting lid for up to 2 weeks.

COCONUT
PUDDING CAKE

There is just something about a coconut cake. The fluffy texture, the white on white on white, the 'furry' exterior. For me, it is the quintessential birthday cake and is a staple on the Violet celebration cakes menu. The filling is based on a classic Hawaiian pudding recipe called Haupia, which is often used in wedding cakes. There is coconut milk in every aspect of this cake so get the best quality one you can find (some canned milks can taste of nothing).

Makes one 20cm (8in) round cake,
to serve up to 12

For the coconut filling:
400g (1⅔ cup) coconut milk
400g (1⅔ cup) coconut milk
100g (½ cup) caster sugar
80g (⅓ cup) water
2 tbsp cornflour dissolved in 3 tbsp
    cold water
⅛ tsp fine sea salt
½ tsp vanilla extract
1½ tbsp white rum

For the coconut soak:
50g (¼ cup) coconut milk
50g (¼ cup) caster sugar
½ tsp vanilla extract
Pinch of salt
2 tsp white rum

For the sponge:
250g (1¾ cups) plain flour
2 tsp baking powder
¾ tsp fine sea salt
85g (¾ stick) unsalted butter, softened
250g (1¼ cups) caster sugar
60g (¼ cup) vegetable oil
2 eggs
160g (⅔ cup) coconut milk
1½ tsp vanilla extract

For the coconut icing:
190g (¾ cup + 2 tbsp) softened
    unsalted butter
750g–1kg (6–8 cups) icing sugar
5 tbsp coconut milk
1 tbsp vanilla extract
2 tsp white rum
Pinch of salt

Desiccated coconut, to decorate

1. First, make the coconut filling. Put the coconut milk, sugar and water into a saucepan. Place over a medium heat, stir to dissolve sugar, then turn up the heat to high.

2. Add the cornflour and water mixture to the pan with the salt and whisk until thick. Pour into a bowl and stir in the vanilla and rum. Let cool then chill for at least 4 hours.

3. Now make the soak. Put the coconut milk, sugar and vanilla into a pan and cook until just about to come to the boil. Leave over a medium heat for 5 minutes, then turn off the heat, add the salt and rum and leave to cool. (This and the filling can be prepared the day before to save time.)

4. Preheat the oven to 150°C fan/170°C/340°F/ gas mark 3½. Grease and line either 1 deep or 3 shallow 20cm (8in) cake tins.

5. Whisk the flour, baking powder and salt together in a bowl and set aside.

6. Put the butter, sugar and oil into the bowl of a stand mixer and cream until light and fluffy. Add the eggs one at a time until combined.

7. Add half of the dry flour mixture to the creamed butter and sugar and mix well. Then add the coconut milk and vanilla and mix again. Scrape down the sides of the bowl and add the remaining dry ingredients to the bowl. Mix well to incorporate all of the ingredients, but do not overmix or this will make your cake tough.

8. Divide the batter between the cake tins and bake for 45–50 minutes, depending on which size tins you are using. The cakes

should be starting to turn golden, feel springy to the touch and a skewer inserted should come out clean.

9. While the cake is baking, make the coconut icing. Put the butter and 500g (2 cups) of the icing sugar into the bowl of a stand mixer and beat until smooth. Stir together the coconut milk, vanilla and rum and gradually add this to the bowl and mix again, scraping the bottom of the bowl as needed. Add another 250g (9oz) icing sugar. Cream together on a low speed for at least 3 minutes (set a timer as 3 minutes is longer than you might think). Add the salt. Gradually add more sugar as needed until you get the right consistency – you want a spreadable and creamy icing that is simultaneously as light as can be. Put a third of the icing into a piping bag with a round nozzle (or use a ziplock/resealable bag and then snip off a corner for a makeshift piping bag). Set aside at room temperature until ready to use.

10. Leave the cakes to cool in their tins, then turn them out onto a wire rack. Wash the tins and line one with a large piece of clingfilm that hangs out over the sides.

11. If you baked the cakes in individual tins, place one layer into the bottom of the lined tin. If you baked the cakes in one deep tin, split it into three layers with a large serrated knife, and put the bottom layer into the clingfilm-lined tin.

12. Soak the bottom layer with a few tablespoons of the coconut soak. Pipe a thick ring of coconut icing around the perimeter of the bottom layer to create a dam for the filling. Fill the middle of the ring with half of the coconut filling.

13. Pipe a couple of stripes of icing across the filling (this serves as a glue for the layers).

14. Add the second cake layer on top of this and then repeat the previous steps before adding the third and final layer of sponge on top. Bring up the overhanging cling film and pop in fridge to chill for a few hours, or overnight.

15. When ready to finish the cake, unwrap it, turn out onto a turntable or cake plate and cover the top and sides with the remaining coconut icing, then lightly press desiccated coconut to cover. See pages 228–9 (the lemon and elderflower cake) for images of the icing method.

ROASTED PLUM and BROWN SUGAR BUTTERCREAM CAKE

My obsession with roasting fruits started when developing the icings for my cupcakes back in 2005. Using jam in cakes is very British – they say the word 'jammy' with a twinkle in their eye. I feel like a cake with jam in it is a harder sell to most Americans. But this is my bid to bring more jam into your life, whichever side of the Atlantic you may be on. Roasting fruit in this way, whether it's plums, rhubarb, quince or apricots, concentrates the flavour quickly without overcooking the fruit.

Makes one three-layer 20cm (8in) cake

For the plums:
1kg (2lb 4oz) plums
1 vanilla pod
100g (½ cup) sugar

For the sponge:
490g (3½ cups) plain flour
4 tsp baking powder
1½ tsp fine sea salt
170g (1½ sticks) unsalted butter, softened
500g (2½ cups) caster sugar
120g (½ cup) sunflower/vegetable oil
4 eggs
320g (1⅓ cups) whole milk
1 tbsp vanilla extract

For the mascarpone filling:
400g (14oz) mascarpone
200g (¾ cup + 2 tbsp) double cream
1 tbsp freshly squeezed orange juice
60g (½ cup) icing sugar, sifted

For the brown sugar buttercream:
900g (2 cups) unsalted butter
9 egg whites (350g)
600g (3⅓ cups) dark brown sugar
1 tsp salt

1. Preheat the oven to 200°C fan/220°C/ 425°F/gas mark 7.

2. Cut the plums into quarters and arrange cut-side up in a roasting tray. Scrape the seeds of the vanilla pod over the plums and tuck the pod between some of the plums as well. Scatter over the sugar, then cover with foil and bake for 15 minutes. Remove the foil and bake for a further 10–15 minutes, or until the plums are starting to fall apart, are catching a little on the edges and are filling your kitchen with that delicious smell. Remove from the oven and allow to cool completely.

3. Reduce the oven temperature to 150°C fan/170°C/340°F/gas mark 3½. Grease and line three 20cm (8in) cake tins.

4. Whisk together the flour, baking powder and salt and set aside.

5. Put the butter, sugar and oil into the bowl of a stand mixer and cream until light and fluffy. Add the eggs one at a time, beating after each addition.

6. Add half of the dry flour mixture to the creamed butter and sugar and mix well. Then add the milk and vanilla and mix well. Scrape down the sides thoroughly and add the remaining dry ingredients to the bowl. Mix well to incorporate all of the ingredients, but do not overmix or this will make your cake tough.

7. Divide the batter between the cake tins and bake for 30–40 minutes. The cakes should be starting to look golden, feel springy to the touch and a skewer inserted should come out clean.

8. While the cakes are baking, prepare the mascarpone filling. Simply whisk all the ingredients together until just fluffy, being careful not to overmix. Keep this in the fridge until ready to use.

9. Next prepare the buttercream. Beat the butter in the bowl of a stand mixer until soft and pale, then set aside. Whisk the egg whites, sugar and salt together in a separate mixing bowl over a bain-marie until the sugar is dissolved, the mixture is frothy and it reaches 75°C/165°F.

10. Fit the bowl to your mixer and whisk until cooled down and stiff peaks form. This can take a little while. You can also turn your mixer off and let it cool a further 20 minutes or so. Switch to a paddle and add the butter in batches, stopping the mixer occasionally to scrape down the sides of bowl. Cover and set aside until ready to use.

11. Once the cakes are completely cool you can begin to assemble the cake. Line a deep 23cm (9in) cake tin with clingfilm, place one layer of sponge inside the lined tin and fill a piping bag with some of the buttercream. Pipe a ring of buttercream around the edge of the cake. Spoon half the mascarpone inside the ring of buttercream and cover with half of the roasted plums, then repeat with the second layer of sponge, border of icing, mascarpone filling, and plums.

12. Place the final layer of cake into the tin and bring the sides of the clingfilm up. Refrigerate the cake for at least an hour and up to 24, this will make it much easier to ice.

13. Remove the cake from the fridge and place onto a plate or stand. Cover the top and sides with the rest of your brown sugar buttercream, using a palette knife.

CALIFORNIA CAKE
(VGN, GF)

This is one of our most popular cakes at Violet, among our vegan and non-vegan customers alike. The mixture of gluten-free flours was chosen for its flavour as much as texture. I wanted to make a vegan and gluten-free cake that was in its own delicious category. In California we are always interested in new ways to eat well and keep our health and bodies happy too. Granted this cake is full of sugar, but it is plant based and gluten free, with that good old-fashioned birthday cake vibe.

Serves 12-15

For the cake:
3 tbsp ground flaxseeds
180g (¾ cup) cold water
210g (1½ cups) sorghum flour
210g (1½ cups) brown rice flour
40g (⅓ cup) tapioca flour
50g (½ cup) ground almonds
1½ tsp xanthan gum
1 tbsp baking powder
1½ tsp fine sea salt
500g (2½ cups) caster sugar
240g (1 cup) sunflower oil
320g (1⅓ cups) almond milk
1 tbsp vanilla extract
½ tsp almond extract
Rainbow sprinkles, to decorate

For the vegan vanilla icing:
500g (4 cups) icing sugar, sifted
190g (¾ cup + 2 tbsp) vegan
  butter, softened
75g (¼ cup + 1 tbsp) almond milk
¼ tsp white vinegar
1 tsp vanilla extract
¼ tsp salt
¼ tsp almond extract

1. Preheat the oven to 150°C fan/170°C/340°F/gas mark 3½. Grease and line a 23×33cm (9×13in) cake tin.

2. Soak the ground flaxseeds in the cold water and set aside for at least 10 minutes before using.

3. In a large mixing bowl, whisk together the flours, ground almonds, xanthan gum, baking powder and salt and set aside.

4. Using a stand mixer fitted with the paddle attachment, beat the sugar and oil together until fluffy. Add the flaxseeds and water and mix well.

5. Add half of the flour mix to the sugar and oil mixture and combine, scraping down the bowl as needed. Add the milk and extracts and mix well before adding the remaining dry ingredients. Mix well to combine.

6. Pour the batter into the prepared cake tin and smooth the top. Bake for 45–50 minutes, or until set and a skewer inserted comes out clean. Remove from the oven and allow the cake to cool completely in the tin before removing. (You can also ice straight into the tin in true sheet cake fashion.)

7. Prepare the icing using a stand mixer or a handheld electric whisk. Combine all of the ingredients and whip for at least 5 minutes until light and fluffy. Spread over the cake and finish with a scattering of sprinkles.

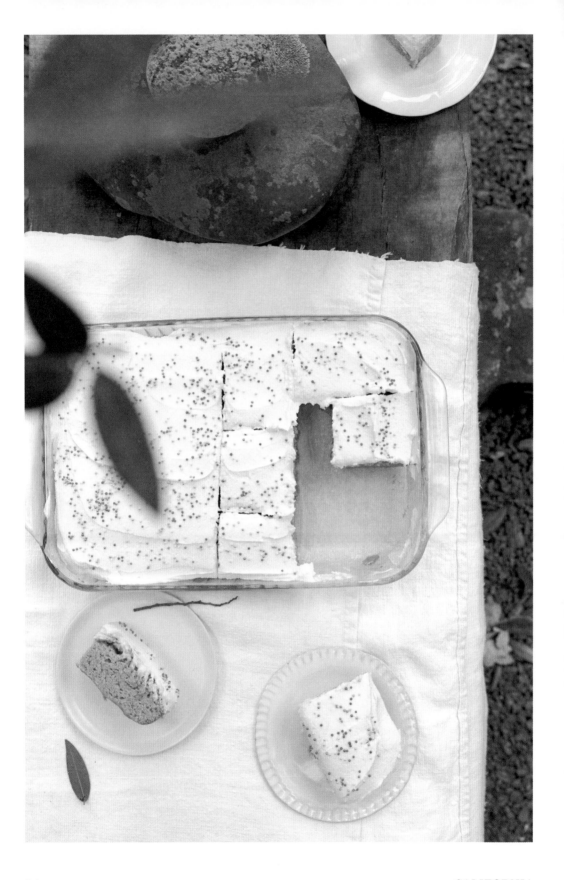

YELLOW CAKE
with CHOCOLATE FROSTING

Classics are classics for a reason. Yellow cake is yellow because of the addition of egg yolks, which both enrich the sponge and add to its flavour. The addition of sour cream (you could use crème fraîche) to the icing makes it tangy and irresistible. Any extra icing keeps well in the freezer.

Serves up to 12

For the cake:
225g (2 sticks or 1 cup) unsalted butter, soft
400g (2½ cups) caster sugar
3 eggs, plus 4 egg yolks
150g (½ cup + 2 tbsp) whole milk
1 tbsp vanilla extract
320g (2 cups + 2 tbsp) plain flour
2 tsp baking powder
½ tsp fine salt

For the icing:
340g (12oz) dark chocolate (70–75% cocoa solids)
240g (1 cup + 1 tbsp) unsalted butter, cut into small pieces
2 tsp vanilla extract
2 tbsp golden syrup
400g (3¼ cups) icing sugar
400g (1½ cups) sour cream
Pinch of salt

1. Preheat the oven to 150°C fan/170°C/ 340°F/gas mark 3½. Grease and line three 20cm (8in) cake tins with baking paper.

2. In the bowl of a stand mixer, cream the butter and sugar until light and fluffy and almost white in colour. Add the eggs one at a time, mixing well after each addition. Add the egg yolks.

3. Combine the milk and vanilla, then set aside.

4. Whisk together the flour, baking powder and salt. Add half the flour mixture to the egg mix, then half the milk, then the other half of the flour followed by the remaining milk, whisking well after each addition.

5. Spoon evenly into the prepared tins, then smooth the tops. Bake for 30–40 minutes, or until the cakes are springy and a skewer inserted into the centre comes out clean. Leave to cool completely in the tins.

6. To make the icing, put the chocolate, butter, vanilla and golden syrup into a heatproof bowl and set over a saucepan of barely simmering water. Stir to combine, then scrape into a food processor and process until cool. Add the icing sugar, sour cream and salt and beat until smooth. Chill for 1 hour. Transfer to a stand mixer and beat with a paddle until creamy and of a spreadable consistency.

7. Once the cakes are completely cool you can begin to assemble the cake. Line a deep 20cm (8in) cake tin with clingfilm, then place one layer of sponge inside the lined tin. Cover with a thick layer of chocolate icing. Repeat with the second layer of sponge and chocolate icing.

8. Place the final layer of cake into the tin and bring the sides of the clingfilm up. Refrigerate the cake for at least an hour and up to 24; this will make it much easier to ice.

9. Remove the cake from the fridge and place onto a plate or stand. Cover the top and sides with the rest of the icing, using a palette knife.

SAVOURIES and HOLIDAY TREATS

CHERRY TOMATO
FOCACCIA

SAVOURIES and HOLIDAY TREATS

I spent a winter back in 2012 baking at the American Academy in Rome. Each morning the pizza bianco would be delivered from a nearby bakery to make sandwiches for the fellows and workers. We would split the very thin focaccia-like bread down the centre and spread half of it with a fresh robiola cheese and the other with greens wilted in chilli and garlic. I make these same sandwiches with my focaccia recipe, dotted with ripe cherry tomatoes, although it's also great just on its own. The best part about this bread is how easy it is. You just let time do the work. No kneading, no shaping.

Serves 6–8

540g (2¼ cups) lukewarm water
4g fast-action dried yeast
   (½×7g sachet)
1 tbsp malt extract or honey
770g (5½ cups) plain flour
1 tbsp fine sea salt
50g (¼ cup) olive oil, plus extra
   for rubbing and drizzling
300g (10½oz) cherry tomatoes
Maldon sea salt, to finish
1 rosemary sprig, leaves picked

For the brine:
¾ tsp fine sea salt
4 tbsp (¼ cup) lukewarm water

1. Pour the lukewarm water into a large bowl, add the yeast and malt extract and stir to dissolve. Tip in the flour, sea salt and 50g (¼ cup) of the olive oil and mix with a wooden spoon until just combined. Resist the temptation to mix it until it is smooth as this can make the bread tough. The dough will be very wet, but it's fine because you just leave it in the bowl to mature and develop on its own. Cover the bowl and allow to rise for 10–12 hours at a cool room temperature. It's best to start this process before bed and bake it in the morning for sandwiches; if you want it with dinner, you'll need to start at 6 a.m.!

2. When your dough has finished maturing (about 10–12 hours), prepare a 25×36cm (10×14in) baking sheet by rubbing it with 2 tablespoons of olive oil. Prepare the brine by mixing the sea salt with the water, then set it aside.

3. Transfer the dough to the oiled baking sheet, then drizzle a little olive oil over the surface as well so that you can push it out into the corners with your fingertips. Leave to rest for 30 minutes and then punch it down with your fingers to create dips all over the dough. Sprinkle the surface with the prepared brine and leave to rest for another 30 minutes.

4. Preheat the oven to 230°C fan/250°C/425°F/gas mark 9 (or the hottest your oven will go).

5. Halve the cherry tomatoes and press them evenly into the dough and then sprinkle with Maldon sea salt and scatter with rosemary leaves. Drizzle with a little more olive oil and bake for 20–25 minutes until golden and bubbly.

POPOVERS

Where I grew up in rural West Marin, there were only about four restaurants to choose from. A taqueria, a pizza place, Manka's Czechoslovakian (where my father was the head waiter) and The Station House Café. It was like a rotation – a couple of nights a month we got to go to one of them. Each place had its merits but The Station House brought you a bread basket. The basket had warm, crumbly cornbread that you would slather with butter, and piping-hot popovers, which are a lot like Yorkshire puddings. They were perfect. This is my best effort at recreating them.

Makes 12 popovers

12 tbsp (¾ cup), vegetable oil plus more
    for greasing
240g (1 cup) semi-skimmed milk
240g (1 cup) water
4 eggs
140g (1 cup) plain flour
1 tsp fine sea salt
A generous grating of nutmeg
A generous grind of black pepper
50g (scant ¼ cup) unsalted butter,
    melted, then cooled

1. Grease a 12-cup muffin tray with oil, making sure you coat the top of the tray as well as the cups. Add 1 tablespoon oil to the bottom of each cup. Set aside.

2. In a jug, whisk together the milk, water and eggs. In a separate large bowl, whisk together the dry ingredients. Slowly add the wet to the dry until it all comes together and there are no lumps. Add the melted and cooled butter, then strain the whole mixture. Let the batter rest for at least 1 hour, but preferably longer, if possible.

3. Put the oiled muffin tin into the oven, set over a roasting tray to catch any drips. When the oil is hot, divide the batter between the cups and bake for 35–45 minutes, or until golden and puffed. They should have tripled in size. Remove the popovers from the tin and drain on kitchen paper for a few minutes before serving. Serve piping hot.

Rich, earthy, unctuous, with a flaky, buttery American biscuit top, savoury cobbler is something I invented for midweek suppers when I haven't got the prep time for proper pastry. Autumn in California is magical, when golden leaves are falling and roadside pumpkin patches and farm stands lure you with their harvesttime treats. There are many squash varieties to choose from, so try something new and see which is your favourite.

Serves 6

For the filling:
1 large squash, such as Crown Prince, Blue Hubbard, butternut or onion squash (about 1.2kg/2lb 10oz)
1 red onion, peeled and cut into 8 wedges
5 tbsp olive oil
1 tsp chilli flakes
6 thyme sprigs
Sea salt and freshly ground black pepper
1 garlic clove, crushed
1×400g (14oz) tin plum tomatoes, drained
200g (¾ cup + 2 tbsp) double cream
10–12 stalks cavolo nero, leaves stripped and stalks discarded

For the topping:
140g (1 cup) plain flour
2 tbsp wholemeal flour
2½ tsp baking powder
1 tsp fine sea salt
150g (1 stick + 3 tbsp) unsalted butter, chilled, cut into 1cm (½in) cubes
4 tbsp plain yoghurt
1 beaten egg, for brushing

1. Preheat the oven to 200°C fan/220°C/425°F/gas mark 7 and line a baking tray with baking paper. You will also need a roughly 20–23cm (8–9in) round or oval ovenproof dish.

2. Peel the squash, slice it in half and scrape out the seeds and pulp. Lay the squash cut-side down and slice it into 1cm (½in) crescents. Spread the squash and onion pieces out on your lined sheet and drizzle with 3 tablespoons of the olive oil. Sprinkle over the chilli flakes, sprigs of thyme, salt and pepper and bake for 20–30 minutes until the squash is tender and the onions are starting to caramelise.

3. Heat the remaining oil in a frying pan over a medium heat and add the crushed garlic. Once it sizzles but before it goes brown, add the drained tomatoes and crush them up a little in the pan. Simmer for about 6–8 minutes, turning the heat down if it bubbles too ferociously. Whisk in the cream. Cut the cavolo nero into ribbons and toss through the tomato sauce. Turn off the heat, gently fold in the roasted vegetables and tip the mixture into your ovenproof dish. Set aside while you make the cobbler topping.

4. In a large bowl, whisk together both flours, the baking powder and salt. Use a pastry cutter, large fork or your fingertips to mix the butter into the flour mixture until you have pea-sized lumps. Stir in the yoghurt and pat the mixture into a ball.

5. On a lightly floured surface, pat out the dough into a circle 2cm (¾in) thick. Use a 6cm (2½in) pastry cutter to get four or five biscuits and then gather the scraps to make the remaining one or two biscuits so that you have six in total. Place the six biscuits on top of the cobbler and brush them with the beaten egg. Bake for 20–25 minutes until the biscuits are puffed and golden and the cobbler is bubbling away. Serve with a green salad.

WHOLE WHEAT
BREAD

Love is a pink cake but it's also sometimes a home-baked loaf of whole wheat bread. Toast can be a lifesaver and having a loaf of this bread always on the go means toast is always at arm's reach. This recipe is adapted from *The Tassajara Bread Book*, written in 1970 by Edward Epse Brown, a Zen priest who also co-founded and ran Greens, a pioneering vegetarian restaurant in San Francisco that has a huge redwood burl sculpture by JB Blunk. Rumour has it the original recipe was created across the dirt road from where we photographed the California portion of this book, in JB's handmade house.

Makes 1 large loaf

For the sponge:
1×7g sachet (1 tsp) fast-action dried yeast
360g (1½ cups) warm water
50g (2 tbsp) malt extract or molasses
385g (2¾ cups) wholemeal flour

For the dough:
2 tsp fine sea salt
55g (½ stick) unsalted butter, softened
280g (2 cups) wholemeal flour

For the egg wash:
1 egg
1 tbsp milk

1. Start by making the sponge. Combine all of the ingredients in the bowl of a stand mixer fitted with the dough hook. (You can, of course, use a bowl, a wooden spoon, and your hands to make this bread, as my mom does.) Cover the bowl with a clean cloth and leave in a warm place (like the laundry room) for 45 minutes, or until doubled in volume.

2. Add the dough ingredients to the sponge base and mix until combined. This could take about 5 minutes in a stand mixer or about 15 if doing by hand. Let the dough rest 10 minutes, then mix/knead again until smooth and elastic for about 5 minutes in a mixer or 15 by hand. Rest a further 10 minutes before giving the dough a final mix/knead. The resting between mixing is key to achieving the correct consistency, so don't rush this step. Cover and allow to rise for a further 60 minutes until doubled in size.

3. Preheat the oven to 160°C fan/180°C/ 350°F/gas mark 4 and butter a 25×12cm (10×5in) loaf tin.

4. Tip out the risen dough onto your worktop. You shouldn't need to flour your worktop as the bread should be nice and elastic; if it is a little tacky, sprinkle over as little flour as possible. Press the dough into a rectangle, roughly 25cm (10in) long and fold it into thirds like a letter and then put into the buttered tin, seam-side down. Leave to prove in the tin for a further 45 minutes in a warm place.

5. Brush the loaf with egg wash, then slit the loaf all the way down the middle with a sharp knife.

6. Bake for 60 minutes in the centre of the oven, until risen, golden and hollow-sounding when tapped. Leave to cool in the tin. This loaf keeps well in a bread tin or covered with a cloth for a few days at room temperature. If you are just using for toast, it can be kept in the fridge in an airtight container for a week.

TEQUILA
PUMPKIN PIE

SAVOURIES and HOLIDAY TREATS

Ahhh, pumpkin pie . . . Thanksgiving wouldn't be Thanksgiving without it. Since moving to London, Fanny Singer and I became the default organisers and chefs of epic Thanksgiving celebrations in London, Cambridge and Cornwall. One year when Fanny was away, her mom Alice Waters was in town but for only 24 hours. We decided to make life easy and meet our friend Malgosia at Gymkhana for an Indian feast to mark the occasion. I did, however, smuggle in this pumpkin pie for dessert which the waiter very graciously laid the table for. The actor Frances McDormand once told me that after a certain age, wine is tricky to process for some women. 'Stick to tequila,' she told me. I've never looked back, and in the process I've discovered some really beautiful tequilas. I especially love the caramel notes in a good Añejo, which is perfect with pumpkin pie. I recommend hunting down Mexican piloncillo brown sugar if possible for this pie too.

Serves 8

½ quantity of chilled pie dough (see page 251)
Flour, for dusting
Whipped cream, to serve

For the filling:
450g (1lb) pumpkin purée
3 eggs
100g (scant ½ cup) double cream
150g (5½oz) piloncillo, grated (or soft light brown sugar)
1 tsp ground cinnamon, plus more for dusting
¼ tsp ground cloves
½ tsp sea salt
3 tbsp maple syrup
2 tbsp good honey
2 tbsp Añejo tequila

Baker's tip: To prepare your own purée, buy a 1kg (2lb 4oz) pumpkin (or squash, such as butternut). Cut it in half, remove the seeds and pulp and bake cut-side down at 180°C fan/200°C/400°F/gas mark 6 for about 30 minutes, or until soft when pierced. Scrape out the cooked flesh and purée in a food processor until smooth. This can kept in the fridge for up to two days or frozen.

1. Remove the pastry from the fridge about 15 minutes before you want to roll it to come to temperature a little. Preheat the oven to 180°C fan/200°C/400°F/gas mark 6.

2. On a lightly floured surface, roll the pastry out to about 2mm thickness and use it to line a deep pie dish. Trim the excess pastry to about 4cm (1½in) and turn this under to create a little ledge. I like to make a simple impression with the back of a fork around the perimeter, but you can also do a traditional crimp. Line the pastry with baking paper and fill with baking beans right up to the top of the pastry. It is important to fill the beans to the top to hold the sides of the pastry up. If you don't have enough dried beans to use, you can also use rice or lentils or any old bag of pulses hanging around in your cupboard. Bake for 20 minutes to set the pastry, then reduce the oven temperature to 140°C fan/160°C/325°F/gas mark 3.

3. Meanwhile, whisk all the filling ingredients together. The pie will be silkier if the pumpkin is as smooth as possible, so if you make your own purée, you will want to push the filling through a fine-mesh sieve. Taste the filling. Adjust the spice if you like it a little spicier. I like to experiment with different levels of heat in the pie. A grinding of fresh black pepper or a pinch of cayenne is delicious, too.

4. Once the pastry is ready, remove the beans and paper from the partially baked pastry and pour in the filling. Smooth the top of the filling then bake in the oven for about 45–50 minutes, or until the custardy filling is just set while retaining a slight wobble.

5. Cool completely before serving – about 3 hours (avoid the fridge as this makes the pastry soggy) – and serve with lightly whipped cream.

RAS EL HANOUT
SNICKERDOODLES

In this adaptation of my mother's recipe, I've swapped the traditional cinnamon with ras el hanout. I first discovered this spice mixture in the souks of Marrakesh, where perfectly precarious pyramids of spices are piled high on makeshift wooden tables throughout the winding narrow streets of the medina. Ras el hanout translates as 'top shelf' and is usually a mixture of the highest quality spices the trader has to offer. Often used in savoury tagines, it also works well in sweet recipes because it is primarily made up of coriander, ginger, nutmeg, turmeric, cloves and dried rose petals.

Makes 15 large cookies

225g (2 sticks or 1 cup) unsalted
    butter, softened
300g (1½ cups) caster sugar
2 eggs
350g (2½ cups) plain flour
1 tbsp ras el hanout
2 tsp cream of tartar
1 tsp bicarbonate of soda
½ tsp fine sea salt

For rolling:
1 tbsp ras el hanout
2 tbsp granulated sugar

Baker's tip: Look for ras el hanout that includes crushed rose petals – these blends are my favourite.

1. Line a small baking sheet or container (one that will fit inside your freezer) with baking paper.

2. Beat the butter and sugar in the bowl of a stand mixer until creamy – you are not aiming for light and fluffy here. Add the eggs and mix well.

3. In another bowl whisk together the flour, ras el hanout, cream of tartar, bicarbonate of soda and salt, then add this to the stand mixer and mix until just combined (do not overmix).

4. Roll individual portions (about the size of a golf ball) of cookie dough and place onto the lined baking sheet or container (they can be touching). Cover and freeze for at least 1 hour, or you can store them in the freezer for up to a month.

5. When ready to bake, preheat the oven to 180°C fan/200°C/400°F/gas mark 6 and line a large baking sheet with baking paper. Let the dough come to temperature a little (10 minutes will do).

6. Mix the ras el hanout and sugar together and roll the balls in the mixture. Arrange the cookies evenly on the sheet, leaving enough space between them so they have room to expand during baking (they will almost double in size).

7. The cookies are best the day or day after they are baked, so it's best to bake them as and when you need them. Bake for 12 minutes, until the centre of each cookie is still slightly soft, but the edges are crisp and golden. Remove from the oven and allow to cool on the tray for 10 minutes before serving.

SAVOURIES and HOLIDAY TREATS

TOM and SHERRY'S GARDEN, INVERNESS, CALIFORNIA

After a long day of shooting for this book we went up to pay a visit to Tom and Sherry Baty. Tom immediately handed me an old wire basket and we walked quietly over to the apple tree to pick Pink Pearls, a California-bred apple with pink flesh and great flavour. We also picked Seckel pears, Meyer lemons, and perfectly ripe peaches from the Magical Peach Tree, so named because it one day grew out of a discarded peach pit in the Batys' compost pile, and because it produces perfect fruits that never bruise as they 'self-harvest' and fall to the ground. Tom thinks the tree may have grown from one the peaches I shared with them during my Chez Panisse days. Perhaps an O'Henry. A lovely thought.

The Batys say fox kits sometimes play with their young cats under the lemon trees and in the raspberry patch. They weren't there the day we were, but a Bambi-like little fawn was happily minding its own business just beyond the garden gate. Lifelong friends of my family, Tom and Sherry were so gracious to let us photograph their favourite place on Earth for my book and to use their produce for the recipes within. I have been visiting this garden for the last 20 or so years with a renewed love and respect since baking became my profession. Tom is an avid fisherman and forager, and Sherry is a long-distance runner who uses the trails and fire roads that splinter off their land on Mount Vision, gathering wild huckleberries along the way. Their love and appreciation for this special part of the world is evident in their garden and on their table. I never leave without a jar of perfectly cured, line-caught tuna, some raspberry jam and a basketful of apples and lemons. If I'm really lucky I get a perfectly rendered jar of lard, made from local hogs. I've been known to smuggle these treasures home to London in my suitcase – cherishing every slice of pie made with home-made Inverness Ridge lard.

ENGI

AND

MORNINGS

FLUFFY
BLUEBERRY MUFFINS

This is the perfect muffin. About half fruit, half muffin, it delivers that intense blueberry hit. Remember, muffins should always be undermixed for the best texture. This keeps them light and fluffy as opposed to dense and tough. When I say undermix, I mean a few lumps and floury bits shouldn't scare you. They work themselves out in the oven.

Makes 10 extra-large muffins

150g (1 stick + 3 tbsp) unsalted butter
200g (1 cup) caster sugar
300g (1½ cups) sour cream
2 eggs
Zest of 1 lemon
Zest of ½ orange
420g (3 cups) plain flour
1 tbsp baking powder
½ tsp bicarbonate soda
¾ tsp salt
430g (3 cups) frozen blueberries

1. Line a large muffin tin with 10 paper cases and grease the top of the tin as these muffins will overflow. Preheat the oven to 180°C fan/200°C/400°C/gas mark 6. Melt the butter in a small saucepan and set aside.

2. In a large bowl, whisk together the sugar, sour cream, eggs and lemon and orange zests until smooth. Whisk a small amount of this mixture into the melted butter to temper it and stop it from seizing up into shards of cold butter. Then whisk in a little more until the butter is cooled completely. Slowly whisk the cooled butter mixture back into the remaining sugar, eggs and sour cream mixture until smooth and incorporated.

3. In a separate bowl whisk together the flour, baking powder, bicarbonate of soda and salt. Add the blueberries and gently toss until coated.

4. Add the wet mixture to the dry; use a rubber spatula to fold together until just combined. It's fine to have small pockets of flour as these will disappear during baking and undermixing gives you a much fluffier muffin.

5. Evenly distribute the mixture between the 10 muffin cups and bake for 35–45 minutes until golden and springy to touch.

FRANNY'S WAFFLES (GF)

My daughter Frances loves waffles as much as I do. I wanted to make them a little more nutritious for her. These are gluten free and you're welcome to make them vegan if you swap out the egg and dairy with your favourite alternatives. We often make these dairy free at home and they are just so delicious.

Makes 6–8 waffles

50g (½ cup) ground almonds
80g (½ cup) brown rice flour
40g (⅓ cup) tapioca flour
1½ tsp baking powder
¼ tsp bicarbonate soda
¼ tsp xanthan gum
¼ tsp salt
1 egg (or egg replacement like milled chia or flaxseeds in water)
160g (⅔ cup) milk (or dairy-free milk)
70g (⅓ cup) strained Greek yoghurt (or dairy-free yoghurt, like coconut)
1 tbsp oil, plus more for greasing
1 tbsp maple syrup

To serve:
Maple syrup
Salted butter
Seasonal fruit like berries or blood orange segments
Greek yoghurt

1. Whisk all the dry ingredients together in a large bowl and set aside. Whisk the wet ingredients together in a jug, then whisk into the dry ingredients.

2. Heat the waffle iron and spray or wipe with oil.

3. Pour the mixture into your waffle iron and cook for 3–5 minutes, or until golden and a little crispy.

4. Serve with maple syrup and salted butter. We also chop up whatever fruit is in season and serve that with it. A little yoghurt would elevate it too.

CHOUX DOUGHNUTS

These doughnuts are as light and airy as a cruller, but look like churros because you pipe them in strips directly into the hot oil. They have an incredible texture because of the choux batter, which is almost creamy in the centre with a subtle crunchy exterior that is enrobed in a tart lemony glaze.

Makes 12 doughnuts

115g (1 stick or ½ cup) unsalted butter, cut into pieces
240g (1 cup) water
¼ tsp fine sea salt
½ tsp caster sugar
175g (1¼ cups) plain flour
3 eggs
1 litre (4 cups) vegetable oil, for frying

You will need a piping bag fitted with a large star tip (e.g. Ateco 868)

For the glaze:
315g (2½ cups) icing sugar
1 tbsp lemon juice
3 tbsp hot water

1. Put the butter, water, sea salt, sugar and flour into a heavy-based saucepan and stir to combine. Place over a medium heat and cook, stirring constantly with a wooden spoon. After 5 minutes the mixture should come together and a film should form on the bottom of the pan. Transfer the mixture to a bowl and set it aside to cool for a few minutes.

2. Add the eggs, one at a time, stirring thoroughly after each addition.

3. Tightly cover the bowl with clingfilm and allow to cool for 10 minutes.

4. Meanwhile, whisk together the glaze ingredients and set aside.

5. Heat vegetable oil in a large, heavy-based saucepan or a deep-fryer to 180°C/350°F and fill your piping bag with the batter. Line a tray with kitchen paper, ready for your fried doughnuts.

6. Pipe lengths of batter straight into the hot oil, a few at a time. Fry until golden, about 7–8 minutes, then transfer to the paper-lined tray to absorb some of the oil.

7. While the doughnuts are still warm dunk into the glaze and place on a baking paper-lined tray to set. Best eaten on the same day.

OLD-FASHIONED DOUGHNUTS

When my friend Liz and I used to hang together after school we would buy a box of six old-fashioned doughnuts from the grocery store and eat the entire lot in one go. They were so simple and so delicious. Cake-style doughnuts are underrepresented in a world saturated with custard and jam-filled re-makes. The dough can be made the day before.

Makes 6 doughnuts

630g (4½ cups) extra-fine sponge
    flour, plus more for dusting
1 tbsp baking powder
200g (1 cup) caster sugar
A couple of gratings of nutmeg
2 tsp fine sea salt
220g (2 sticks or 1 cup) unsalted
    butter, cold, cut into 1cm (½in) dice
4 egg yolks
300g (1½ cups) plain yoghurt
Vegetable oil, for frying

For the glaze:
1 tbsp lemon juice
1 tbsp vanilla extract
1 tbsp hot water
400g (3¼ cups) icing sugar
½ tsp salt

You will need a 9cm (3½in) and a 3cm
    (1¼in) round pastry cutter

1. In the bowl of a stand mixer sift together the flour, baking powder, sugar, nutmeg and salt. Add the butter and mix until you have a coarse meal.

2. In a separate bowl whisk together the egg yolks and yoghurt, then add to the stand mixer and mix until the dough comes together.

3. Turn the dough out on to a piece of clingfilm, wrap tightly and chill for 2 hours.

4. Dust a work surface liberally with flour, then roll the chilled dough out to a thickness of 2cm (¾in) and cut out as many doughnuts as you can using the 9cm (3½in) round cutter. Pat the scraps together and reroll one more time to get about 6 doughnuts in all. Use a 3cm (1¼in) round cutter to cut out the holes (keep these and fry and glaze them as you do the doughnuts). Score lines on top of each doughnut in a pentagonal pattern.

5. Pour vegetable oil into a heavy-based saucepan or deep-fryer and heat to 180°C/350°F. Fry the doughnuts for 4–5 minutes on one side (until golden), and then for 2–3 minutes on the second side, or until evenly golden. Transfer to a tray or plate lined with kitchen paper to absorb any excess oil.

6. To make the glaze, mix together all of the ingredients in a shallow bowl; if it is too thick you can add a little more hot water.

7. Dip the warm doughnuts into the glaze, then put on a wire rack to cool with a tray underneath to catch the drips.

CHOCOLATE GLAZED DOUGHNUTS

This recipe has a step or two but it is entirely worth the effort. The fact that it takes so long to make is like a built-in firewall to stop you eating them every day.

Makes 12 doughnuts

1×7g sachet (1 tsp) fast-action
    dried yeast
50g (¼ cup) caster sugar
120g (½ cup) lukewarm water
490g (3½ cups) strong white bread
    flour
2 tsp fine sea salt
3 eggs
125g (1 stick + 1 tbsp) unsalted
    butter, cut into 1cm (½in) pieces
1 litre (4 cups) vegetable oil, for frying
Chocolate sprinkles or cacao nibs, for
    sprinkling (optional)

For the chocolate glaze:
300g (11oz) dark chocolate (70–75%
    cocoa solids), finely chopped
180g (¾ cup) double cream
120g (½ cup) sour cream or crème
    fraîche
180g (¾ cup) water
4 tbsp (¼ cup) caster sugar
2 tbsp vanilla extract
1 tsp fine sea salt

You will need a 9cm (3½in) and a 3cm
    (1¼in) round pastry cutter

1. In the bowl of a stand mixer fitted with a dough hook, dissolve the yeast and sugar in the warm tap water. Add the flour and salt and mix to form a dough. Add the eggs one by one, and beat for about 10 minutes. Add the pieces of butter one by one, until fully incorporated into the dough. Cover the bowl loosely with clingfilm and leave to rise for about 2 hours, or until doubled in size. Punch down, then re-cover and chill overnight.

2. When you are ready to make your doughnuts, use a dough scraper or spatula to turn the chilled dough out onto a liberally floured surface. Sprinkle the dough with flour and roll out into a 2cm (¾in) thick square.

3. Use a 9cm (3½in) round cutter to cut as many rounds as you can, then use the 3cm (1¼in) cutter to cut holes out of the centre of each round to make a doughnut. Re-roll the scraps for the remaining doughnuts. Do not reroll a second time but you can fry off the scraps and dust them with icing sugar!

4. Carefully place the doughnuts onto floured baking trays, leaving plenty of space between them. If you don't have enough trays, you could use floured plates. Leave to rise 45 minutes; meanwhile, make the glaze.

5. Put 200g (7oz) of the chopped chocolate into a small heatproof bowl. Heat the double cream in a small saucepan until it just starts to foam and steam – watch that it doesn't boil over. Pour the hot cream over the chocolate, leave to sit for 10 minutes, then stir until smooth.

6. Wash out the saucepan used to heat the cream, then add the remaining chocolate, sour cream or crème fraîche, water,

caster sugar, vanilla extract and salt. Set over a medium-low heat, whisking periodically until all the ingredients have melted. Increase the heat to medium-high and cook for 5 minutes more, to thicken the sauce slightly. Remove from the heat and whisk into the chocolate ganache mixture. (Occasionally this mixture can appear broken or split, but it is easily brought back together with a stick blender or blitzing in your food processor.) Leave in a warm place away from draughts until ready to use. If your glaze gets too cold and thick, you can place it over a pot of boiling water for a few minutes to melt it again.

7. Have ready kitchen paper-lined trays. Heat the vegetable oil in a large, heavy-based saucepan or a deep-fryer to 180°C/ 350°F. Use a clean pastry brush to dust off as much flour as possible from the doughnuts before dropping them carefully into the hot oil a few doughnuts at a time, being careful not to overcrowd the pot. Fry for 5 minutes on one side, then flip over and fry the other side until golden, about 2 more minutes. Lift the doughnuts out of the hot oil with a spider strainer or tongs and place on the kitchen paper to soak up any oil.

8. Prepare a wire rack by placing over a baking tray lined with fresh baking paper. While your doughnuts are still warm, dunk them one by one into your melted chocolate glaze. I like to fully immerse them on both sides to completely cover the doughnuts with glaze, but one side will do.

9. Set the glazed doughnut on the prepared wire rack. You can reuse any glaze that falls onto the lined baking tray underneath, so that nothing is wasted. Sprinkle with cacao nibs or chocolate sprinkles, if you like.

CHOCOLATE VIOLET
BABKA BUNS

Dark chocolate and violet is a magical combination – elegant, unexpected and special. This is a perfect bun to make in February when violets are popping up – if you're lucky enough to find some growing nearby, pick them and sprinkle them over the finished buns.

Makes 6 buns

3.5g (½×7g sachet) fast-action
    dried yeast
25g (2 tbsp) caster sugar
4 tbsp (¼ cup) lukewarm water
280g (2 cups) strong white flour
1 tsp fine sea salt
2 eggs
65g (¼ cup + 1 tbsp) unsalted butter,
    cut into 1cm (½in) pieces

For the filling:
100g (1 cup) hazelnuts
115g (1 stick) chilled unsalted butter
150g (¾ cup + 1 tbsp) brown sugar
175g (6oz) 70% dark chocolate
50g (½ cup) cocoa powder
2 tbsp violet syrup (see page XVII)
¼ tsp fine sea salt

For the syrup soak:
100g (½ cup) caster sugar
120g (½ cup) water
1 tbsp honey
Pinch of salt
1 tbsp violet liquor

1. In the bowl of a stand mixer fitted with a dough hook, dissolve the yeast and sugar in the warm water. Add the flour and salt, and mix to form a dough. Add the eggs one by one, and beat for about 10 minutes. Add the pieces of butter one by one, until fully incorporated into the dough. Cover the bowl loosely with clingfilm and leave to rise for about 2 hours, or until doubled in size. Punch down then re-cover and chill overnight.

2. Meanwhile, make the filling. Start by toasting the hazelnuts on a baking sheet in a hot oven for 7–10 minutes until golden. Place into a clean tea towel and rub off the papery skins. Chop finely.

3. Measure the butter, brown sugar, chocolate, cocoa powder and violet syrup into a saucepan and place over a medium-low heat, whisking continuously until all the ingredients have melted together. Set aside.

4. On a lightly floured surface, roll the dough out into a rectangle about 40×60cm (16×24in). Use a sharp knife to cut the dough into 6 strips, each 40×10cm (16×4in). Spread each strip of dough with chocolate then sprinkle with the hazelnuts and salt. Roll each strip into logs, then slice lengthways down the middle to reveal the filling, leaving one end intact.

5. Carefully twist the two log halves around each other in a rope-like fashion. You will lose some of the filling here, but don't worry. Then roll each twist into a little knot.

6. Cover loosely with clingfilm, and leave to rise for 2 hours, or until doubled in size.

7. Preheat the oven to 160°C fan/180°C /350°F/gas mark 4 while you make the syrup soak. Put all of the ingredients into a small saucepan, simmer gently until melted together, then set aside.

8. Transfer the babka buns to a baking sheet lined with baking paper and bake for 35–40 minutes, or until a skewer inserted comes out clean. Remove from the oven and pour the syrup over the babka buns while they are still hot. It is a lot of syrup, but don't worry, the babka will take it. Leave to cool slightly before serving.

135 MORNINGS

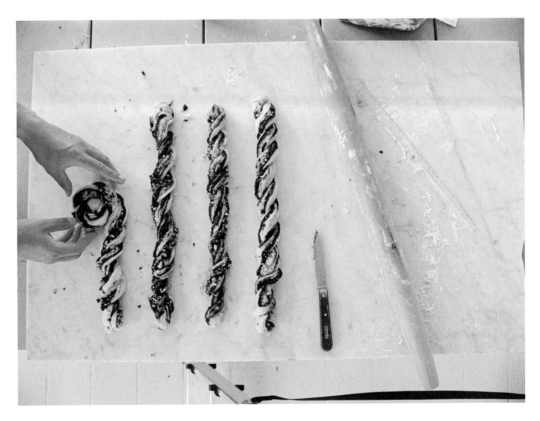

ENGLAND

FERN VERROW FARM: A BIODYNAMIC FARM
in the ENGLISH COUNTRYSIDE

Having moved to London, I was desperate to make relationships as special as the ones I had with the people at Frog Hollow and many other California farms, so I went to the historic Borough Market in Southwark. I quickly realised this market was more about green-grocers than farmers. Greengrocers are wonderful in England. They take great care to choose the freshest fruits and vegetables from the many different distributers and farms in the UK, as well as from Italy, France, Spain and beyond.

There was, however, one farmer. At her stall, in the middle of an abundance of flowers and fruit, I met Jane Scotter from Fern Verrow, a 16-acre biodynamic farm in Herefordshire. The philosophy behind biodynamic farming begins with a series of lectures given in the 1920s by Austrian thinker Rudolf Steiner. Farmers were concerned about the loss of fertility in soil even 100 years ago, and his principles included farming without pesticides and chemical fertilisers. Farms generate their own fertility through composting, which makes for better, more delicious crops, and creates a healthy ecosystem for other living things on the farm. This is something that is tangible when walking through Fern Verrow's glasshouses, with their sprouting trays of saved seeds and hillside of raspberry and strawberry bushes bursting with red fruit. Jane also grows some of the most beautiful and unique varieties of flowers for cutting: hydrangea, roses, lilies and Sweet William to name but a few.

When I first asked if I could visit her farm Jane said, with brilliant British politeness, 'At the risk of sounding rude, no.' I learned people do things differently over here. But her fruits and vegetables were like nothing else I'd seen in England, and I was determined to find a way to convince her I wasn't just a tourist. Eventually, I ended up selling my cakes in a market stall right next to Jane's, at Spa Terminus in Bermondsey, getting deliveries of her produce to the bakery and (in 2015) styling her cookbook *Fern Verrow: Recipes from the Farm Kitchen* on location at the farm. Jane's fruits quite literally inspire and influence my work. If it were not for her loganberries, blackcurrants and whitecurrants the recipes for 'Summer Pudding Sundae' (page 149) and 'Strawberry and Whitecurrant Coconut Meringue Cake' (page 163) would not exist. She grows jostaberries, a cross between gooseberries and black-currants, which are in my matcha cake (page 173). I have never seen them anywhere else in the world. My intention in including these unusual fruits is to get you out there trying different, less popular varieties at your own farmer's markets and greengrocers. Supermarkets will sell produce with the longest shelf life and so many farms (understandably) grow long-lived varieties for this reason, rather than for flavour. Many farms and distributors, like the wonderful Natoora, who we use for the bakery in London, work alongside small producers in order to get these flavour-driven crops to market quickly and efficiently. But a few years back Jane made the exciting decision to work directly with Chef Skye Gyngell and her restaurant Spring in London. Jane grows just for them (and the few lucky enough to get the excess, like us and Jeremy Lee at Quo Vadis).

AFTERNOONS

NECTARINE and CHERRY COBBLER

Unlike a traditional cobbler, this one has a 'bottom', which makes it more like a cobbler sandwich. It's excellent with nectarines and cherries but you could use peaches or plums too. A perfect bake for a summer picnic.

Serves 8

For the bottom:
115g (1 stick or ½ cup) unsalted butter, softened
100g (½ cup) granulated sugar
1 tsp fine sea salt
2 eggs
280g (2 cups) plain flour
1 tsp baking powder
120g (½ cup) milk

For the fruit filling:
3–4 white nectarines, stoned and cut into eighths
200g (7oz) cherries, pitted and halved
90g (½ cup) brown sugar
1 tsp lemon juice

For the topping:
210g (1½ cups) plain flour
1 tbsp sugar
1 tbsp baking powder
½ tsp fine sea salt
150g (1 stick + 2 tbsp) butter, cut into 1cm (½in) pieces
1 egg
60g (¼ cup) milk
45g (¼ cup) demerara sugar

1. Preheat the oven to 170°C fan/190°C/ 375°F/gas mark 5. Butter and line a 23×33cm (9×13in) baking tray with baking paper.

2. For the bottom, cream together the butter, sugar and salt until light and fluffy, in a stand mixer fitted with the paddle attachment. Add the eggs one at a time until incorporated. Whisk together the flour and baking powder, then add half to the butter, sugar and eggs. Once mixed, add half the milk, followed by the remaining flour, then the remaining milk. Mix until smooth but not overmixed. Spread the mixture into your lined tin, and smooth the top with a spatula.

3. For the fruit filling, put the nectarines, cherries, sugar and lemon juice into a bowl and toss together. Leave to macerate while you prepare the topping.

4. Put the flour, sugar, baking powder and salt into the bowl of a food processor and pulse to combine. Add the butter and process until the mixture is a sandy texture. Add the egg and milk and pulse a few times to bring the dough together.

5. The fruit should now be well macerated, so toss it again in the sugar and juices. Tip the fruit and any juice over the base mixture, spreading it evenly.

6. Drop spoonfuls of the topping mixture over the fruit, leaving some fruit exposed in a cobbler pattern. Sprinkle with the demerara sugar and bake for 25–30 minutes, or until golden and cooked through.

This recipe was born out of having an abundance of these amazing currants and berries from Fern Verrow Farm. While shooting this book, we made a gigantic batch of the filling for the brioche buns (see page 152) after our pilgrimage to the farm and I suddenly thought: let's make ice cream with the leftovers! I think it's my new favourite ice cream flavour.

Makes 4 sundaes

For the summer pudding filling:
100g (¾ cup) blackcurrants, stalks removed
100g (¾ cup) redcurrants, stalks removed
50g (¼ cup) whitecurrants (or more redcurrants), stalks removed
50g (¼ cup) caster sugar
1 tbsp lemon juice
125g (¾ cup) raspberries
½ vanilla pod, slit lengthways
4–6 rose geranium leaves

For the ice-cream base:
2 egg whites
100g (½ cup) caster sugar
1 tsp golden syrup
Pinch of salt
150g (½ cup + 2 tbsp) double cream
1 heaped tbsp plain yoghurt

To serve:
240g (1 cup) double cream, whipped
Redcurrants, whitecurrants and raspberries
Caster sugar, for sprinkling
Leftover fruit syrup, for drizzling (optional)

1. Put the blackcurrants, redcurrants and whitecurrants in a saucepan with the sugar and lemon juice. Scrape the seeds from the vanilla pod into the saucepan, then add the empty pod too. Cook over a low heat for 3–4 minutes, stirring gently until the sugar dissolves. The currants will release their juices but don't let them cook for too long – you want to keep the flavours bright. Remove the pan from the heat, fish out the vanilla pod and set it aside for rinsing and drying (or simply discard it). Stir in the raspberries and leave them for 10 minutes to melt into the hot currants. Add the geranium leaves, then put into the fridge to chill until ready to use. It's best to chill overnight for maximum flavour.

2. Strain the fruit from the syrup, reserving both parts. Using a stick blender or food processor, blitz the strained berries until smooth, adding half of the syrup back in. Push this purée through a sieve to get rid of any seeds. You will need about 250g (9oz) of this smooth purée to fold into your ice-cream base, so add more of the syrup/liquid if needed. Set aside while you make the base.

3. Put the egg whites, caster sugar, golden syrup and salt into a heatproof bowl, then place this bowl over a small saucepan of simmering water (making sure the base of the bowl does not touch the water). Whisk continuously until the sugar has dissolved and the mixture starts to become frothy and opaque. If you have a sugar thermometer, use it to bring the mixture up to 75°C (167°F). Remove from the heat and use a hand-held electric whisk to make stiff peaks of meringue. Cool completely.

4. In a large clean bowl, whip the cold double cream and yoghurt to very soft peaks. Fold in the meringue, just to combine, then fold in the fruit purée.

5. Pour the mixture into your ice-cream machine and churn following the manufacturer's instructions. I tend to under-churn a little so as not to make the ice cream too icy. Chill in the freezer at least 1 hour before making your sundaes.

6. To assemble, scoop the ice cream into tall glasses or sundae coupes and top with whipped cream and fresh berries sprinkled with a little caster sugar. If you have any of the purée or poaching liquid left you could drizzle that over the top as well.

I love the flavours of summer pudding but I don't love the soggy bread. This is a deconstructed summer pudding with fresh brioche buns, which you could also buy from a really good bakery if you don't feel like making them from scratch. You will need a stand mixer to make the brioche because it is important to keep the butter from melting as it is incorporated into the dough. This recipe makes 12 buns because when making brioche dough it seems silly to just make 6. If you don't want 12 buns you could use half the dough to make a brioche loaf.

Makes 12 buns

115g (1 stick or ½ cup) unsalted butter
270g (1 cup + 2 tbsp) whole milk
14g (2 sachets) fast-action dried yeast
100g (½ cup) caster sugar
490g (3½ cups) strong flour
1 tsp salt
2 eggs
1 egg yolk
2 tbsp double cream
2 tbsp demerara sugar

For the filling:
200g (1¼ cups) blackcurrants, stalks
    removed
200g (1¼ cups) redcurrants, stalks
    removed
100g (½ cup + 2 tbsp) whitecurrants
    (or more redcurrants), stalks
    removed
150g (¾ cup) caster sugar
1 tbsp lemon juice
1 vanilla pod, split lengthways
500g (3 cups) raspberries
About 8 rose geranium leaves
480g (2 cups) double cream

Baker's tip: Rose geraniums are one of the easiest plants to grow in pots in just about any sunny spot you can find. Cut it back and bake with the leaves and it will keep coming back, year after year. You will want the rose variety for the best flavour, which also has lovely little pink flowers in summer.

1. Cut 75g (5 tbsp) of the butter into 1cm (½in) cubes, and leave to soften to room temperature. Use the remaining butter to generously butter a large bowl.

2. Warm the milk in a small saucepan over a medium heat until lukewarm. Stir the yeast and caster sugar into the milk and let the yeast bloom for a few minutes.

3. Put the flour and salt into the bowl of a stand mixer fitted with a dough hook. Add the yeast mixture and mix until a dough forms, about 5 minutes. Now add the eggs one by one, mixing fully after each addition. Mix on a medium speed for 5–10 minutes until the dough comes away from the sides and is starting to get elastic.

4. At this point you can start adding the soft butter, one piece at a time. Continue until all of the butter is fully incorporated into the dough. The dough will feel slightly sticky. Turn into the buttered bowl, loosely cover with clingfilm, and leave for about 2 hours, or until doubled in size.

5. After 2 hours knock back the dough, then cover tightly with clingfilm and chill in the fridge for at least 6 hours, or overnight. This chills the butter in the dough, which allows you to shape it.

6. While the dough is chilling you can prepare the filling. Put the blackcurrants, redcurrants and whitecurrants into a saucepan with the sugar and lemon juice. Scrape the seeds from the vanilla pod into the saucepan, then add the empty pod too. Cook over a low heat for 3–4 minutes, stirring gently until the sugar dissolves. The currants will release their juices but don't let them cook for too long – you want to keep the flavours bright. Remove the pan from the heat, fish out the vanilla pod and set it aside for rinsing and drying (or simply discard it). Stir in the raspberries and leave them for 10 minutes to melt into the hot currants. Add the geranium leaves, then put into the fridge to chill until ready to use. It's best to chill overnight for maximum flavour.

7. Take your chilled dough from the fridge and line a baking sheet with baking paper. If you want to make a small brioche loaf instead of 12 buns lightly butter a 12×18cm (5×7in) loaf tin.

8. Divide the dough into 12 pieces (or shape half the dough into 6 pieces and the other half into 3 pieces for the loaf). Shape each

piece into a ball and place on the lined baking sheet, seam-side down. If making a loaf, place the three larger pieces into your prepared loaf tin. Cover the buns (and loaf, if making) with clingfilm and leave to rise for 45 minutes. Fifteen minutes before the buns are done rising, preheat the oven to 180°C fan/200°C/400°F/gas mark 6.

9. Whisk together the egg yolk and cream and brush this over the buns (and loaf, if making). Sprinkle the demerara sugar over the top and bake for 25–35 minutes, until puffed and golden. Allow the buns to cool completely on the baking sheet.

10. When ready to serve, whip the double cream to soft peaks. Make an incision in each bun and spoon in a generous amount of the fruit filling and then spoon a dollop of cream on top. Serve immediately.

ENGLAND

CHOCOLATE ALMOND
MACAROON TEACAKES (GF)

This was created out of the memory of a bite of a 'Sarah Bernhardt cake', bought at The Village Mall in Corte Madera around 1990. I think it was in a bakery called Cocolat. I remember the moment I bit into this treasure – I can even remember the robin's egg blue colour on the walls and the smell of melted chocolate. Nothing else. This is a recipe with many parts and I recommend a piping bag and a sugar thermometer, although they can be made without them.

Makes 12 teacakes

For the almond macaroon base:
50g (⅓ cup) flaked almonds
75g (¾ cup) ground almonds
175g (¾ cup + 2 tbsp) caster sugar
1 tbsp cornflour
2 egg whites
½ tsp almond extract

For the marshmallow:
1 egg white
50g (¼ cup) caster sugar
1½ tsp golden syrup
Small pinch of fine salt
½ tsp almond extract

For the chocolate ganache:
200g (7 oz) dark chocolate,
    roughly chopped
240g (1 cup) double cream

To finish:
50g (1/3 cup) flaked almonds,
    lightly toasted

1. Preheat the oven to 150°C fan/170°C/340°F/gas mark 3½ and line a large baking tray with baking paper.

2. Mix the flaked and ground almonds, 100g (½ cup) of the caster sugar and the cornflour together and set aside. Put the remaining sugar, egg whites and almond extract into a clean bowl and whisk together to form soft peaks. Fold the two mixtures together, then spoon 12 circles of the mixture onto the lined tray and flatten slightly with the back of a spoon. Bake for 20 minutes, then carefully peel off the paper and allow to cool on a wire rack.

3. For the marshmallow, put all the ingredients into the metal bowl of your stand mixer and set over a saucepan of simmering water (do not let the water touch the bottom of the bowl or it will cook the egg whites). Whisk continuously by hand with a balloon whisk, until the sugar dissolves and the mixture is very warm to the touch. If using a sugar thermometer, whisk continuously for 2 minutes, or until it reads 70–75°C (158–167°F) – whichever comes first. Transfer the bowl to your electric mixer (fitted with the whisk attachment) and whisk quickly until stiff peaks are just beginning to form.

4. Put the mixture in a piping bag with a large round nozzle. Pipe large bubble shapes onto your cooled macaroons (or use a spoon).

5. To make the ganache, put the chocolate into a heatproof bowl. Heat 200g (scant ¾ cup) of the cream until just beginning to bubble, then pour it over the chocolate. Let it sit for 10 minutes, then stir until smooth. If the ganache is a little broken or split, stir in the remaining cold cream until smooth.

6. Position the wire rack of macaroons over a baking paper-lined tray, to catch any chocolate drips. Spoon the chocolate over the marshmallow macaroons, coating them evenly. Top with the flaked almonds, then leave to set for 15 minutes before serving.

DOUBLE CHOCOLATE
SEA SALT COOKIES
(GF)

The combination of flours used makes
these cookies gluten free, as well as
lending them a gooey-chewy texture.
Be sure to underbake these cookies as
directed or they become dry. Best eaten
warm when the chocolate is molten.

Makes 9 large cookies

70g (½ cup) rice flour
35g (¼ cup) sorghum or gram flour
2 tbsp milled flaxseeds
½ tsp xanthan gum
50g (½ cup) cocoa powder
¾ tsp flaky sea salt
½ tsp baking powder
¼ tsp bicarbonate of soda
100g (generous ½ cup) brown sugar
75g (⅜ cup) caster sugar
100g (scant ½ cup) unsalted butter,
    at room temperature
½ tbsp vanilla extract
2 eggs
100g (3½oz) dark chocolate
    (70% cocoa solids), chopped

1. Preheat the oven to 170°C fan/190°C/
   375°F/gas mark 5 and line a baking sheet
   with baking paper.

2. In a mixing bowl whisk together the
   rice flour, sorghum flour, milled flaxseeds,
   xanthan gum, cocoa powder, sea salt,
   baking powder and bicarb and set aside.

3. In the bowl of a stand mixer fitted with
   the paddle attachment, cream the two
   sugars with the butter until smooth
   and light. Add the vanilla and eggs and
   beat well, then scrape down the sides
   of the bowl and beat again. Add the dry
   ingredients and the chocolate pieces
   and beat until combined.

4. I like to use an ice-cream scoop to
   portion out the cookies. For cookies that
   you plan to bake and eat straight away,
   place balls of dough on the lined baking
   sheet about 10cm (4in) apart. Bake for
   9–10 minutes until the cookies are crisp
   on the outside but still soft in the middle.
   They will seem a little underdone,
   but remember they will continue to cook
   slightly as they cool.

5. For cookies that you want to save for
   another day, scoop the mixture into balls
   while it is still soft and place them on
   a tray or in a container that will fit in your
   freezer. Freeze for up to 3 months; to
   use just remove from the freezer and bake
   from frozen at a moment's notice (they
   may take a little longer in the oven).

CHOCOLATE MARSHMALLOW
WHOOPIE PIES

This recipe was first published in my cookbook *The Whoopie Pie Book*, back in 2011. It is a very cute, fun book that we turned around in about four months, at the same time I was opening Violet on Wilton Way. Whoopies are still one of my go-to picnic cakes, wrapped up in baking paper and packed into a picnic basket.

Makes about 9 large or 24 mini whoopie pies

175g (1¼ cups) plain flour
100g (1 cup) unsweetened cocoa powder
1½ tsp bicarbonate of soda
½ tsp baking powder
½ tsp salt
125g (½ cup + 1 tbsp) unsalted
    butter, softened
200g (1 cup) sugar
1 egg
225g (1 cup) buttermilk
1 tsp vanilla extract

For the marshmallow filling:
3 egg whites
150g (¾ cup) caster sugar
2 tbsp golden syrup
Pinch of salt
1 tsp vanilla extract

1. In a bowl, sift together the flour, cocoa powder, bicarb and baking powder. Stir in the salt and set aside.

2. In a separate bowl, cream the softened butter and sugar together until light and fluffy, using an electric hand-held whisk or a stand mixer fitted with the paddle attachment. Add the egg and mix well, then add the buttermilk and vanilla and beat until well combined. Slowly add the dry ingredients in two batches, mixing until just incorporated. Chill the batter for 30 minutes before using so that it is easier to scoop.

3. Preheat the oven to 160°C fan/180°C/350°F/gas mark 4 and line 2 baking trays with baking paper.

4. Drop 18 large or 48 small scoops of batter, about 5cm (2in) apart, onto the prepared baking trays. Bake on the middle shelf of the oven for 10–12 minutes for large whoopies or 8–10 minutes for mini whoopies, until the pies are left with a slight impression when touched with a finger. Remove from the oven and transfer to a wire rack to cool completely while you make your marshmallow filling.

5. Fit your stand mixer with a whisk attachment. Put all the ingredients into the metal bowl of your mixer and set over a saucepan of boiling water (do not let the water touch the bottom of the bowl or it will cook the egg whites). Whisk continuously until the sugar dissolves and the mixture is very warm to the touch. If you are using a thermometer, heat the mixture, whisking continuously for 2 minutes, or until it reads 70–75°C (158–167°F) – whichever comes first. Transfer the bowl to your electric mixer and whisk on high speed until just beginning to form stiff peaks.

6. To assemble: spread or pipe a generous scoop of marshmallow filling onto the flat surface of a cooled whoopie. Top with another whoopie to make a sandwich, then serve.

APRICOT, CHAMOMILE and HONEY SCONES

I've never been a huge fan of chamomile tea, but it's one of my favourite baking flavours, particularly as vanilla is so ubiquitous. I especially love it paired with apricots – they harmonise to be greater than the sum of their parts. Add clotted cream and a perfectly buttery scone and it's difficult to do better.

Makes 6 large scones

For the compote:
1kg (2lb 3oz) firm, ripe apricots, halved
    and stones removed
½ vanilla pod
1 tbsp dried chamomile flowers
    (or 2–3 teabags, opened, depending
    on size)
150g (¾ cup) caster sugar

For the scones:
280g (2 cups) plain flour
1 tbsp baking powder
2 tbsp caster sugar
½ tsp fine sea salt
115g (1 stick) chilled unsalted butter,
    cut into 1cm (½in) cubes
100g (scant ½ cup) double cream
100g (scant ½ cup) whole milk

For the egg wash:
1 egg white, beaten
2 tbsp milk
2 tbsp caster sugar

Clotted cream to serve (or use whipped
    cream or mascarpone)
Honey, for drizzling

1. First make the compote – put all the ingredients into a large bowl and toss together well. Macerate for 1 hour to dissolve the sugar and draw the juices out of the fruit.

2. Tip into a heavy-based saucepan and cook over a low heat for 15 minutes, or until the apricots have broken down a bit. Allow to cool and then transfer to a container to chill in the fridge. This will keep for about 2 weeks in the fridge.

3. Preheat the oven to 170°C fan/190°C/ 375°F/gas mark 5 and line a baking tray with baking paper.

4. In a food processor, combine the flour, baking powder, sugar and salt, then add the cold butter, blitzing until it resembles a coarse meal texture. (You can also do this by hand with a pastry cutter.)

5. Drizzle in the cream and milk, mixing until the dough just comes together (be careful not to overmix). Turn out onto a lightly floured surface, pat into a cube shape and leave to rest for 10 minutes.

6. Once rested, roll to a thickness of 2cm (¾in), then cut into 6cm (2½in) rounds and place on a tray. Chill for 20 minutes in the freezer, then remove and transfer to your lined baking tray. Whisk together the egg wash ingredients and brush this over the chilled scones. Bake for 15–20 minutes until springy and golden at the edges.

7. Allow the scones to cool slightly before filling with compote and a dollop of the cream. Add a drizzle of honey and serve immediately.

STRAWBERRY
and WHITECURRANT COCONUT
MERINGUE CAKE

You don't see meringue cakes around that much but I challenge you to make them popular again. Like a pavlova with substance, the sponge at the bottom soaks up all the cream and berry juices in a beautiful way.

Serves 10–12

125g (½ cup + 1 tbsp) unsalted
    butter, softened
175g (¾ cup + 2 tbsp) caster sugar
50g (¼ cup) soft light brown sugar
2 tsp vanilla extract
2 eggs
210g (1½ cups) plain flour
80g (1 cup) desiccated coconut
½ tsp fine sea salt
1½ tsp baking powder
400g (1⅔ cup) coconut milk

For the meringue:
4 egg whites
2 tsp vanilla extract
½ tsp cream of tartar
200g (1 cup) caster sugar

For the topping:
1kg (2lb 4oz) strawberries
Few drops of angostura bitters
1 tsp vanilla extract
1 tbsp caster sugar
560g (2 cups) double cream
125g (½ cup + 2 tbsp) crème fraîche
icing sugar, for dusting
200g (1¼ cup) whitecurrant
    (or redcurrant) sprigs

1. Preheat the oven to 170°C fan/190°C/ 375°F/gas mark 5 and butter and line a 20×30cm (8×12in) baking tin or Swiss roll tin, leaving enough paper to overhang on two of the sides.

2. To make the cake, cream the butter and sugars together until light and fluffy. Add the vanilla and eggs and mix well.

3. In a separate bowl whisk together the flour, coconut, salt and baking powder and set aside.

4. Add half of the coconut milk to the butter mixture and combine well, then add half of the dry ingredients and mix again. Mix in the remaining coconut milk and then the remaining dry and mix well, then pour the cake batter into the lined tin and smooth over.

5. Now make the meringue. Put the egg whites, vanilla and cream of tartar into a spotlessly clean bowl and whisk until frothy. Gradually add the sugar and whisk on high speed until stiff peaks form. Spread this on top of the cake batter, leaving a rough surface. Bake in the oven for 35–40 minutes, or until the cake is golden and set. Remove from the oven and allow the cake to cool in the tin for 10 minutes, then gently remove from the tin, using the baking paper to lift it out. Carefully peel the paper away from underneath the cake as you transfer to a serving plate.

6. Hull the strawberries and cut some in half and some in quarters. Add to a bowl and sprinkle with the bitters, vanilla and sugar; toss together and set aside.

7. Whip the double cream and crème fraîche to soft peaks and spread over the top of the cake and then top with the strawberries. Dust over some icing sugar, finish with the whitecurrant sprigs and serve right away.

ENGLAND

MARBLE CAKE

I love this cake. I have to give a shoutout to Miami chef Oscar Lastra, who is really the one who came up with the idea. Oscar and I chatted about recipes on Instagram a fair amount over lockdown. We never met, but we bonded over cake and music in the early days of Covid, when he posted a photo of a marble cake made from my lemon drizzle recipe because of how much he liked the texture. This is exactly how recipes are born, from a search for the perfect texture combined with the perfect flavour. I hope mine is as good as his looked.

Serves 6–8

265g (2 sticks + 2 tbsp)
    unsalted butter, very soft, plus
    extra for greasing
265g (1⅓ cups) caster sugar
3 eggs
2 tsp vanilla extract
265g (1¾ cup + 4 tsp) plain flour
120g (½ cup) boiling water
1½ tsp baking powder
1 tsp fine sea salt
80g (⅓ cup) buttermilk
75g (¾ cup) cocoa powder

For the icing:
160g (1¼ cups) icing sugar
2 tbsp hot water
85g (3oz) white chocolate, melted
    and cooled

1. Preheat the oven to 170°C fan/190°C/375°F/gas mark 5 and butter and line a large loaf tin, about 25×10cm (10×4in), with baking paper. Make sure the paper comes up the sides of the tin.

2. Put the butter and sugar into the bowl of a stand mixer and cream together well, but not as fluffy as you would for a layer cake. Beat in the eggs, one at a time, mixing well after each addition. Mix in the vanilla.

3. Whisk together the flour, baking powder and salt in a large bowl. Mix in half of this flour mixture, scraping down the sides as you go, until barely combined. Keep the mixer going while you add the buttermilk.

4. Add the remaining flour and mix until just combined, then scrape down the bowl and give it one last mix.

5. Spoon one third of the mixture into a bowl and set aside. Whisk together the cocoa powder and boiled water until smooth and stir this into the reserved cake mixture until it's incorporated.

6. Dollop both cake mixtures into the prepared tin, starting with a layer of plain mixture and then adding alternating dollops of chocolate mixture to look like a checkerboard. Run a knife through the batters in a swirling motion to create a marble effect. Less is more here, so resist the temptation to over-swirl.

7. Bake in the oven for 50–60 minutes, or until springy and a skewer inserted comes out clean. Leave to cool in the tin.

8. In a small bowl whisk together the icing sugar, hot water and cooled melted white chocolate until smooth.

9. Remove the loaf from the tin by running a small knife around the sides of the tin, then tilting the tin on its side and coaxing the loaf out, using the baking paper as a handle. Remove the paper and turn the loaf upright on your wire rack. Drizzle over the icing and let it drip down the sides, then carefully transfer to a serving dish.

ENGLAND

Different to the American Angel Food Cake (see page 63), Frances and I discovered this pink and yellow English corner shop classic after swimming lessons one evening and fell in love at first sight. The buttercream filling is salty with a hint of almond extract which makes it taste old-fashioned and delicious.

Makes 12 cakes

500g (2½ cups) caster sugar
80g (⅓ cup) oil
175g (1½ sticks or ¾ cup) unsalted
    butter, softened
4 eggs
1 tbsp vanilla extract
Yellow food colouring
Pink food colouring
490g (3½ cups) plain flour
1 tbsp + 1 tsp baking powder
1 tsp fine sea salt
360g (1½ cups) milk

For the buttercream filling:
115g (1 stick or ½ cup) unsalted
    butter, softened
⅛ tsp salt
¼ tsp apple cider vinegar
    (or white wine vinegar)
1 tsp vanilla extract
⅛ tsp almond extract (optional,
    but highly recommended)
250g (2 cups) icing sugar
2 tbsp double cream

1. Preheat the oven to 150°C fan/170°C/ 340°F/gas mark 3½ and grease and line two 23×33cm (9×12in) rectangular cake tins.

2. Beat the sugar, oil and soft butter together until light and fluffy. Add the eggs and vanilla and mix well. Now divide this mixture between two bowls. Add pink food colouring to one bowl and yellow to the other – it's best to make it a little darker than you would think as the flour will dull the colour.

3. Whisk together the flour, baking powder and salt and set aside. Divide the milk between the two bowls and mix well, then divide the dry ingredients between the two bowls and use a wooden spoon or mixer to combine into a smooth batter.

4. Pour the yellow batter into one tin and the pink into the other. Bake for 45 minutes, or until springy and a skewer inserted comes out clean. Leave to cool completely in the tins.

5. Meanwhile, make the buttercream filling. Put the butter and salt into a bowl with the vinegar, vanilla and almond extracts and half of the icing sugar and beat well with a hand-held electric whisk to get a creamy consistency. Add the cream and mix well, then add the rest of the sugar and beat on medium speed for 5 minutes. (Set a timer as 5 minutes feels like a long time but you really need the full 5 minutes to get the correct texture.)

6. To assemble, remove the cooled cakes from their tins by flipping out onto a cooling rack or board. Carefully peel away the baking paper from the bottoms and trim any domes with a serrated knife so the cakes are identical in height.

7. Cover one of the cakes with the buttercream and sandwich the other cake on top. Dipping a sharp knife briefly into hot water to make a clean cut, wiping and dipping again for each cut, to give a clean line, trim the sides to reveal the bright colours and slice into 12 identical slices. Place in cupcake cases or paper doilies and serve.

ENGLAND

BROWN SUGAR
VICTORIA SPONGE

This golden brown, less refined version of Victoria sponge has a wonderful texture. I love it with my quick strawberry jam – strawberries and brown sugar are very good friends. A layer of whipped unsweetened cream in the middle balances out the cake perfectly.

Makes 1×20cm (8in) cake, to serve 8–10

For the quick strawberry jam:
250g (10½oz) strawberries, hulled and
  quartered (cut smaller if the berries
  are very large)
225g (1¼ cups) demerara or raw sugar
Juice of 1 lemon
Pinch of salt

250g (2 sticks + 2 tbsp) unsalted
  butter, at room temperature
250g (1¼ cups) brown sugar
4 eggs
250g (1¾ cups) plain flour
1 tbsp baking powder
½ tsp salt

To assemble:
150g (5½oz) quick strawberry jam
230g (1 cup) double cream
Icing sugar, for dusting

1. First make the jam. Put 125g (3½oz) of the strawberries with half of the sugar into a small heavy-bottomed pot and crush with a potato masher (or similar) while warming through over a low heat.

2. Preheat the oven to 180°C fan/200°C/400°F/gas mark 6 and line a roasting tin with baking paper. Put the remaining sugar into the lined roasting tin and bake in the oven for 10–15 minutes to warm through.

3. Add the remaining strawberries and sugar to the crushed strawberries, bringing just to a simmer, then add the warm sugar. The warm sugar keeps the cooking going swiftly so you can cook the fruit as quickly as possible, preserving that fresh fruit taste. Stir until the sugar dissolves, then add the lemon juice. Bring to the boil and allow to bubble away for 12–15 minutes. Cool completely (any leftovers after the cake has been assembled will keep for up to 2 weeks).

4. Preheat the oven to 150°C fan/170°C/340°F/gas mark 3½ and grease and line two 20cm (8in) cake tins with baking paper.

5. In the bowl of a stand mixer fitted with the paddle attachment, cream the butter and sugar together until pale and fluffy. Beat in the eggs one at a time, beating between each addition and scraping down the sides of the bowl as needed.

6. Whisk the flour, baking powder and salt together, then add this to the mixer and continue to mix just until incorporated.

7. Divide the mixture evenly between the prepared cake tins, then bake on the middle shelf of the oven for 25–30 minutes, or until a skewer inserted in the centre comes out clean. Leave to cool in the tins before turning out.

8. Once the cakes are cool, spread one cake with 150g of the cooled jam. Whip the cream to soft peaks and spoon on top of the jam, then top with the second cake layer. Dust with icing sugar. Chill until ready to serve to keep the cream nice and fresh.

ENGLAND

COFFEE WALNUT CAKE
with FERNET

Coffee walnut cake is found in just about every museum café in England, for better or for worse. It can often be a little too sweet and a little too dry but there is no denying that the pleasing bitterness of coffee and walnuts are perfect together. I love the herbaceous quality of Fernet, a bitter aromatic Italian spirit, and I think its addition here cuts the sweetness of the icing and adds another level of flavour.

Serves 10–12

350g (3 sticks + 1 tbsp) unsalted butter, softened
350g (1¾ cups) soft light brown sugar
5 eggs
250g (1¼ cups) walnuts
280g (2 cups) plain flour
1 tbsp baking powder
1 tsp sea salt
120g (½ cup) brewed espresso
4 tbsp Fernet

For the espresso buttercream:
4 tbsp (¼ cup) cold espresso
2 tbsp double cream
185g (1½ sticks + 1 tbsp) unsalted butter
2 tbsp Fernet
750g–1kg (3–4 cups) icing sugar

1. Preheat the oven to 150°C fan/170°C/340°F/gas mark 3½ and grease and line three 20cm (8in) cake tins with baking paper.

2. In a stand mixer fitted with the paddle attachment, cream together the butter and light brown sugar until pale and fluffy. Add the eggs one at a time, mixing well after each addition.

3. Set aside a couple of walnuts for decoration, then chop the rest medium fine, leaving some chunky bits for texture. Add them to the butter mixture and mix until just combined.

4. In a separate bowl, whisk together the flour, baking powder and salt, then mix this into the butter mixture until just combined. Add the brewed espresso and Fernet and mix until smooth.

5. Divide the mixture evenly between the three tins and smooth the tops, then bake for 35–40 minutes until risen and springy to touch and a skewer inserted in the centre comes out clean. Leave to cool completely in the tins.

6. While the cakes are baking, prepare the buttercream. Wash out the bowl of your mixer to use it again. Add all of the ingredients except the icing sugar to the bowl and mix well, then add up to 750g (3 cups) icing sugar in two batches to avoid mess. Mix for 5 minutes (set a timer as this is longer than it seems). If the icing is soft add the remaining 250g (1 cup) icing sugar.

7. Line one of your cake tins with clingfilm and place a layer of the cake inside. Spread with a quarter of the icing. Place the next layer on top and repeat. Top with the last layer of sponge. Cover the cake with clingfilm and chill in the fridge for at least 30 minutes. Unwrap the cake and turn it out onto a cake plate. Ice the top of the cake. You usually see this cake with exposed sides, which is quite cute. You can ice the sides if you prefer or leave them exposed, but either way, decorate by grating walnut over the top with a microplane zester or other sharp grater.

JOSTABERRY
and LOGANBERRY
MATCHA CAKE

I've only ever seen a jostaberry on Jane Scotter's Fern Verrow Farm. I did consider whether I should include these berries in a recipe as you may never have the opportunity to try one, but then I can't pretend that these delicious berries don't exist! They are a kind of cross between a blackcurrant and a gooseberry so use a combo of these instead if you can't get jostas – and if you can't get those, use rasp-berries and blackberries. I love the colours and the flavour of bitter matcha tea in this cake. With all that caffeine, this is a great afternoon pick-me-up.

Makes 1 large cake

230g (1 cup) unsalted butter
350g (2½ cups) plain flour
1½ tsp baking powder
½ tsp bicarbonate of soda
½ tsp fine sea salt
2 tbsp matcha powder
3 eggs
200g (1 cup) caster sugar
300g (1½ cups) plain yoghurt
1 tbsp vanilla bean paste
Icing sugar, for dusting
Cream, to serve (optional)

For the fruit topping:
250g (9oz) jostaberries (or any
    combination of gooseberries,
    blackcurrants and blackberries)
250g (9oz) loganberries
    (or raspberries)
100g (½ cup) caster sugar

1. Preheat the oven to 170°C fan/190°C/ 375°F/gas mark 5 and line a 25cm (10in) springform or loose-bottomed cake tin with baking paper.

2. First prepare the fruit topping: clean and remove any stems from the berries, then place into a bowl with the sugar and set aside to macerate.

3. Melt the butter and set aside to cool slightly.

4. In a bowl measure out the flour, baking powder, bicarbonate of soda, salt and matcha powder, whisk together and set aside.

5. In another bowl, whisk together the eggs and sugar until smooth and then whisk in the yoghurt and vanilla until combined. Slowly whisk a small amount of the egg mixture into the melted butter to temper it. Then whisk this butter into the remaining egg mixture until a smooth batter forms.

6. Pour the wet mixture over the dry flour, mix and whisk until just combined – do not overmix. Pour the batter into the prepared tin and scatter the macerated berries over the top. Bake the cake on the middle shelf of the oven for 40–45 minutes, or until springy to touch. Allow to cool for a few minutes before removing from the tin.

7. The cake can be served right away or at room temperature, dusted with icing sugar, and with cream if liked, but is best served on the day it is made.

BAKEWELL BARS

The Violet Bakewell Bar has become another classic. It is baked in a tray, like a blondie or brownie, and sits on a layer of shortbread rather than shortcrust pastry. We also change the preserves seasonally. I love it with a cherry or apricot preserve in the summer, although if you want to stick to the classic Bakewell use raspberry jam, or use the recipes for homemade strawberry or blackberry jam on pages 170 and 86.

Makes 12 bars

For the base:
250g (1¾ cups) plain flour
100g (¾ cup) icing sugar
½ tsp salt
200g (¾ cup + 2 tbsp) unsalted butter, cold, cubed
200g (7oz) good-quality cherry jam

For the topping:
200g (¾ cup + 2 tbsp) unsalted butter, softened
200g (1 cup) golden caster sugar
¼ tsp almond extract
½ tsp vanilla extract
¼ tsp fine sea salt
2 eggs + 1 egg white
150g (¾ cup) whole almonds (skin on), roughly chopped
50g (⅓ cup) plain flour
1½ tsp baking powder

To decorate:
3 tbsp fresh lemon juice
300g (2½ cups) icing sugar
Preserved cherries like Amarena or Luxardo

1. Preheat the oven to 180°C fan/200°C/400°F/gas mark 6. Butter and line an 18×30cm (7×12in) baking tin with baking paper.

2. For the shortbread base, combine the flour, icing sugar, salt and butter in a food processor and blitz until the mixture has just come together into a ball. Press the pastry evenly into the prepared tin. Bake for 20 minutes until golden brown, then remove from the oven and reduce the temperature to 160°C fan/180°C/350°F/gas mark 4. Let the base cool for 10 minutes before spreading the jam gently over the top.

3. For the topping, beat the butter and sugar together until creamy but not fluffy. Add the extracts, salt, eggs and egg white, then beat well.

4. Stir in the chopped almonds, flour and baking powder just to combine. Dollop this over the jam – don't worry about spreading it evenly as it will melt into place in the oven and spreading it can cause the jam to get mixed in rather than remaining its own layer. Return to the oven for 30–40 minutes, or until golden and set. Allow to cool for 20 minutes.

5. Meanwhile, whisk together the lemon juice and icing sugar until smooth. Spread this glaze over the cooled Bakewell, then slice into fingers. Decorate each slice with a preserved cherry.

6. These will keep well in an airtight container for up to 5 days.

TAHINI HALVA BROWNIES

These have become a staple at Violet. Every once in a while we give them a little break from the counter to make space for other recipes, but it never lasts long because people ask for them every day. Halva can be found in many Turkish and Middle Eastern shops or online.

Makes 12 brownies

250g (1 cup + 2 tbsp) unsalted butter
250g (9oz) dark chocolate
4 eggs
250g (1¼ cups) golden caster sugar
2 tsp vanilla extract
140g (1 cup) fine spelt flour
50g (½ cup) cocoa powder
150g (5½oz) tahini paste
225g (8oz) vanilla or marbled chocolate
    halva, broken into 2cm (¾in) pieces
¾ tsp sea salt flakes

Baker's tip: Remember that both brownies and cookies continue to bake while they cool down. It is always a good idea to err on the side of caution and remove the baked goods just before you think they are done to avoid overbaking and to keep that lovely gooey texture.

1. Preheat the oven to 160°C fan/180°C/350°F/ gas mark 4. Butter and line a 20×30cm (8×12in) cake tin with baking paper.

2. Put the butter and chocolate into a heat-proof bowl set over a pan of simmering water, making sure the base of the bowl doesn't touch the water. Stir occasionally until the mixture has melted completely. Set aside to cool slightly.

3. In a separate bowl, whisk the eggs and sugar until combined, taking care not to overwhisk; the idea here is not to add too much air. Stir the eggs into the cooled chocolate mixture with the vanilla extract, then sift in the flour and cocoa powder and fold all together. Pour into your prepared tin.

4. Drizzle the tahini over the top of the brownie mixture. Dot with halva pieces, then gently run a knife across the surface to marble it. Sprinkle with sea salt, then bake for 25 minutes. The brownies should be just set but still wobbly. Leave to cool in the tin before cutting into rectangles.

AFTER a MEAL

CHOCOLATE CREAM PUFFS

I've always been more cream puff than profiterole. I used to buy the supermarket ones, which are soggy and too sweet but still so moreish. There's something about the salty choux filled with sweet cream and dripping in chocolate sauce that gets me every time. Here is the real deal.

Makes about 18–20 cream puffs

For the glaze:
150g (5½oz) dark chocolate
    (70% cocoa solids)
150g (½ cup + 2 tbsp) double cream
2 tbsp caster sugar
100g (scant ½ cup) water
1 tbsp vanilla extract
½ tsp fine sea salt
50g (¼ cup) sour cream or
    crème fraîche

For the puffs:
240g (1 cup) water
120g (1 stick + 1 tbsp) unsalted butter
½ tsp fine sea salt
1 tsp caster sugar
140g (1 cup) plain flour
4 eggs
Beaten egg, for brushing

For the cream:
600g (2½ cups) double cream
4 tbsp caster sugar
1 tbsp vanilla extract

1. Line a large baking sheet (or two smaller ones) with kitchen paper and set aside.

2. First make the glaze. Take 100g (3½oz) of the chocolate and chop into small pieces, then transfer to a small bowl. Heat the double cream in a small saucepan until just below boiling point, or until it starts to foam and steam (watch that it doesn't boil over). Remove the pan from the heat and pour over the chocolate. Let sit for 10 minutes to melt, then stir until smooth – this is the ganache mixture.

3. Wash out the pan used to heat the cream and add the remaining chocolate along with the caster sugar, water, vanilla extract, salt and crème fraîche. Heat over a medium-low flame, whisking periodically until all the ingredients have melted. Turn up to medium-high and cook for 5 minutes more, to thicken the sauce slightly. Remove from the heat and whisk into the chocolate ganache. Occasionally this mixture can appear broken or split, but it is easily brought back together with a stick blender or by blitzing in your food processor. Leave in a warm place away from draughts until ready to use. If your glaze gets too cold and thick, you can place it over a pan of boiling water for a few minutes to melt it again.

4. Preheat the oven to 180°C fan/200°C/ 400°F/gas mark 6.

5. To make the puffs combine all of the ingredients except the eggs in a heavy-based saucepan. Place over a medium heat and stir constantly with a wooden spoon for a few minutes until the mixture comes together and makes a film on the bottom of the pan. Transfer to a bowl and let it cool for a couple of minutes. Start adding the eggs, one at a time, stirring

181

AFTER a MEAL

thoroughly after each addition. The mixture will seem slimy and like the eggs won't incorporate, but continue stirring and they will.

6. Once all of the eggs are added, use two spoons to scoop the mixture onto your lined baking sheets. Use one spoon to get a nice golf-ball-size blob of dough and the other to scrape it off and onto your baking sheet. Space them about 4cm (1½in) apart to give them room to puff up.

7. Brush the tops with the beaten egg wash and bake for about 30 minutes until golden and puffed. Remove from the oven and then use a bamboo skewer (or sharp knife) to pierce each puff, releasing the steam. Leave to cool completely on the sheet.

8. When you are ready to serve, whip the cream to soft peaks with the sugar and vanilla. Slice each puff in half, fill with the sweetened whipped cream. Then place the puffs on a wire rack over a lined baking tray to catch the drips before pouring the chocolate sauce over the top.

BUTTERSCOTCH PUFF-PUFFS

I used to live around the corner from a great little West African restaurant in London called Banke's Kitchen. I first tried puff-puffs, admittedly, because the name is so cute, but I have become obsessed with the simple, sweet, yeasty fried dough. You could roll them in caster sugar or dip them like I do in caramel but they are usually served as they are, plain, as a snack.

Makes about 12 puff-puffs

490g (3½ cups) plain flour
14g (2 sachets) fast-action dried yeast
200g (1 cup) caster sugar
480g (2 cups) water
1 tsp vanilla bean paste, or the
    scraped seeds of 2 vanilla pods
    plus 1 tsp vanilla extract
2 litres vegetable oil, for frying

For the butterscotch sauce:
300g (1¼ cups) double cream
½ vanilla pod, slit lengthways
60g (¼ cup) golden syrup
500g (2½ cups) sugar
120g (½ cup) water
1 tsp flaky sea salt
1 tbsp lemon juice
125g (1 stick + 1 tbsp) chilled
    unsalted butter, diced

1. Thoroughly combine all the puff-puff ingredients, except the oil, in a bowl with a whisk (or use a stand mixer), then cover and let rest for 2 hours.

2. Meanwhile make the butterscotch sauce. Warm the cream and scraped vanilla seeds (and the pod) over a medium heat. Set aside but keep warm.

3. Heat the golden syrup, sugar, water and sea salt in a large, high-sided saucepan. Bring to the boil until it turns dark golden and almost looks burnt.

4. Transfer the warm cream to a jug and remove the vanilla pod, then whisk into the pan of caramel in a slow, steady stream. It will bubble up a lot so work carefully and slowly.

5. Once all the cream has been added, whisk in the lemon juice, then whisk in the butter chunks one at a time. Leave the caramel to one side to cool.

6. To cook the puff-puffs, pour the vegetable oil into a large, heavy-based saucepan or deep-fryer and heat to 190°C (370°F). Have a plate ready with some kitchen paper to soak up some of the excess oil.

7. Use an ice-cream scoop to add dollops of dough to the hot oil, being careful not to overcrowd the pan. Wait for them to puff, then flip over with a slotted spoon. Keep turning in the hot oil until they are evenly golden brown, then drain on kitchen paper. Repeat until you have about 12 puffs, stirring the batter each time before you drop into the oil.

8. Serve the hot puff-puffs immediately, alongside the caramel sauce.

AFTER a MEAL

TREACLE TART
with WHIPPED CREAM

The first time I tasted this very British dessert was at St. John Bread and Wine almost 20 years ago. It's very rich, but fantastic on occasion. I love the chewy texture and the hint of lemon in the butterscotch-y filling. I add a dash of vodka to mine in order to cut the sweetness down a little. You can play with the citrus here and use mandarin, Meyer lemon, or even lime. I have tried to make it with various types of bread – sourdough is a no-no. I love it with a pain de mie best. Treacle tart is also Cockney rhyming slang for 'sweetheart' – I think this is the cutest.

Serves 8

For the pastry:
140g (1 cup) plain flour
⅛ tsp fine sea salt
½ tsp caster sugar
115g (1 stick or ½ cup) unsalted butter, chilled and diced
2 tbsp iced water

For the filling:
200g (1¾ cups) fresh breadcrumbs from a slightly stale loaf of white bread
800g (2¼ cups) golden syrup
Juice of 1 large lemon, lime, orange or mandarin
2 tsp vanilla extract
1 tbsp vodka (optional)
½ tsp flaky sea salt

Unsweetened whipped cream, to serve

1. First grease a 25cm (10in) loose-bottomed tart tin. Put the flour, salt and sugar into a food processor and blitz to combine. Add the cold butter and pulse until it resembles coarse breadcrumbs. Drizzle in the iced water (you may not need it all) just until it comes together into a ball. Press the dough into a disc, wrap in cling-film and chill in the fridge for 20 minutes.

2. Lightly flour a work surface and turn the dough out onto it. Roll it out into a 28cm (11in) circle. Carefully lift and lower this into the tart tin, pressing it gently to line the base and sides of the tin. Trim off any excess dough, then chill in the fridge or freezer for at least 30 minutes, or until ready to use.

3. Meanwhile prepare the filling. Tip the breadcrumbs into a large bowl, add the remaining ingredients and stir well. Set aside to allow the bread to soak up the syrup. Meanwhile, preheat the oven to 180°C fan/200°C/400°F/gas mark 6.

4. When ready to bake, loosely cover the case with a piece of baking paper and fill with ceramic baking beans or dried beans. Bake for 15 minutes, then remove the paper and beans and return to the oven for another 10 minutes until the pastry is golden brown.

5. Tip the filling into the hot tart case; it should come near to the edge of the pastry. Cook for a further 25–30 minutes until the filling has set and turned a light toffee shade. Allow the tart to cool before removing from the tin. Serve with unsweetened whipped cream.

FIG LEAF GRILLED
RED PEACHES
(GF)

These are a favourite summer creation and best done outside on the barbecue. I like to cook with a hot fire at the start of the meal for searing meat or to bring a cauldron of beans to a boil and then move the coals around to cook the meat or vegetables more slowly. Once dinner is ready to serve there is usually just the right amount of heat left to grill these simply garnished peaches. If you don't have a barbecue, you can also bake them in the oven, so don't despair. While they cook the peaches absorb the coconutty flavour of the fig leaves, adding to their complexity.

Serves 6 hungry eaters or 12 after
a large meal

12 fig leaves
6 ripe round red peaches, or another
    small variety
1 lemon
70g (5 tbsp) unsalted butter
1 small egg yolk
2 tsp amaretto
50g (½ cup) ground almonds
50g (1¾ oz) amaretti cookies
1 tbsp caster sugar, plus more
    for sprinkling

Baker's tip: Fig trees grow all over both England and California. They are often huge and abundant with leaves in the summer. I highly recommend finding a nice one and helping yourself to the low-hanging leaves.

1. Light your barbecue; alternatively preheat the oven to 180°C fan/200°C/400°F/ gas mark 6.

2. Wash and dry the fig leaves and set them out on a baking sheet.

3. Halve the peaches and remove the pits. Place a peach half, cut-side up, on top of each fig leaf and squeeze lemon juice over them.

4. Add the remaining ingredients to a blender or food processor and blitz to make a coarse paste. Using two spoons, add a heaped spoonful of this almond filling to the centre of each peach half. Sprinkle with a little sugar so that the flesh has a thin layer.

5. Place the peaches in their fig leaves directly onto the grill, or on a baking sheet and into the oven, if using. Cook for about 20–30 minutes, or until the peaches are tender and infused with fig leaf perfume but still holding their shape. If cooking in the oven, the tops should get a little charred and bubbly. If cooking on the barbecue the cooking time will depend on how hot the fire is so keep an eye on them.

AFTER a MEAL

PEACH LEAF
ICE CREAM
(GF)

People have been cooking and baking with leaves forever, but they are still seldom seen on menus. The leaf of a peach tree has a very special bitter almond quality, not unlike marzipan, but the flavour has a green quality to it, a freshness. It is important not to over-steep the leaves. When cooked too long, the flavour will go vegetal and unpleasant.

Serves 4

3 egg yolks
360g (1½ cups) double cream
240g (1 cup) whole milk
75g (⅜ cup) caster sugar, plus more
  to taste
2 large handfuls of peach leaves,
  roughly 40 leaves
Pinch of salt

Baker's tip: Getting peach leaves is admittedly not the easiest, even for me. But they are so special and remind me of both England and California so I really wanted to include them in this book. My advice is to go to a farmer's market where they sell peaches and ask the farmer to bring you some branches the following week. You just might be in luck!

1. Put the egg yolks into a medium bowl and whisk to break them up. Set aside. Measure the double cream into a large bowl or container with a sieve resting on top of it and set aside.

2. In a heavy-based pan, warm the milk and sugar until just beginning to bubble. Drop a third of the peach leaves into the milk for 30 seconds to steep, then remove with a small sieve or spider strainer and discard. Add the remaining leaves for a further 30 seconds, then repeat and discard. You are basically making a delicate infusion.

3. When the milk is pale green and fully steeped with the peach leaves, temper the yolks by pouring a little of the milk into them, whisking as you go. Now pour the tempered yolks back into the remaining warm milk in the pan. Stirring continuously with a wooden spoon or heatproof rubber spatula, heat until the mixture just starts to thicken at the bottom of the pan. Lift the spoon or spatula up periodically to check this. Strain the custard through the sieve into the cold cream and whisk well to prevent the custard from cooking any further.

4. Taste the mixture and add a pinch of salt or sugar as needed. As freezing dulls the sweetness of ice cream, the mixture should be slightly sweeter than you want the finished product to be.

5. Pour the mixture into an ice-cream machine and churn for about 20 minutes, following the manufacturer's instructions. Freeze for 1 hour before serving.

AFTER a MEAL

BLACKCURRANT and VIOLET SORBET (GF)

Violet syrup can be found online, and it is something we use daily at the bakery. Ours comes from France and is different to violet liqueur or violet extract. This sorbet is dark and green in flavour, yet delicate and sweet. Excellent on its own or in a sundae with any of the other ice creams in this chapter.

Serves 6

300g (1½ cups) caster sugar
120g (½ cup) water
900g (2lb) blackcurrants,
    stems removed
4 tbsp violet syrup

Baker's tip: If you don't have an ice-cream machine, you can make granita instead, by putting the mixture into a shallow container in your freezer and whisking every 30 minutes until you have a beautiful, slushy granita.

1. First, make a sugar syrup. Put 250g (1¼ cups) of the caster sugar and the water into a small saucepan and place over a medium heat, stirring occasionally until dissolved. Turn off the heat, drop in the blackcurrants and cover with a lid for at least 2 hours.

2. Strain the blackcurrants, reserving both the syrup and the pulpy fruit. Purée the blackcurrant pulp with the remaining 50g (¼ cup) caster sugar, then push through a sieve back into the blackcurrant syrup, removing as many seeds as possible. Stir in the violet syrup and taste. This is the one time you want something to taste a little too sweet, because this sweetness will fade when the mixture is frozen. If it is still too tart, add sugar to taste. If the violet is not strong enough, add a little more violet syrup.

3. Pour the mixture into an ice-cream machine and churn according to the manufacturer's instructions.

GREENGAGE
ICE CREAM
(GF)

Greengages are a dessert plum known for their perfect balance of tart and sweet. I love the colour too. Plums are ideal for ice cream because their complex flavours really shine through. You could substitute any ripe plum or pluot here if greengages are not available.

Serves 8

For the custard:
175g (¾ cup) whole milk
150g (¾ cup) caster sugar
½ vanilla pod, slit lengthways
2 egg yolks
325g (1⅓ cups) double cream

For the greengages:
500g (1lb 2oz) greengage plums, sliced
    and pitted
½ vanilla pod, slit lengthways
100g (½ cup) water
50g (½ cup) sugar, plus more to taste
2 tsp kirsch
Pinch of salt

1. In a heavy-based pan, warm the milk, caster sugar and vanilla pod until just beginning to bubble. This won't take long, so while it's heating up, put your egg yolks into a bowl and whisk to break them up. Pour the double cream into a large bowl with a sieve resting on top of it and set aside.

2. When the milk is ready, temper the yolks by pouring a little of the warm milk into them, whisking as you go. Now pour the tempered yolks back into the remaining warm milk in the pan. Stirring continuously, heat until the mixture starts to thicken at the bottom of the pan. Strain the custard mixture into the cold cream and whisk well to prevent the custard from cooking any further. Cover and put in the fridge for at least 1 hour to cool.

3. Put the plums into a saucepan with the vanilla, water and sugar and cook over a medium heat until the fruit begins to break down. Cool slightly and purée, then transfer to the fridge to cool completely.

4. Once the purée has cooled, stir it into the ice cream custard base. Taste the mixture and add the kirsch and a pinch of salt or sugar as needed. As freezing dulls the sweetness of ice cream, the mixture should be slightly sweeter than you want it to be.

5. Pour the mix into your ice-cream machine and churn for about 20 minutes, or following the manufacturer's instructions. Depending on the size of your machine you may have to do this in a couple of batches. Freeze for 1 hour before serving.

RASPBERRY LOGANBERRY ROULADE with MASCARPONE (GF)

Roulades are retro. You don't see them enough in the US but they have a pretty good stronghold in the UK. This version is light and soft, swirled with creamy mascarpone and punctuated with ripe tart summer raspberries and loganberries. If you don't have loganberries, substitute blackberries. All three components meld together in perfect berry harmony.

Serves 6–8

For the meringue:
4 egg whites
250g (1¼ cups) caster sugar
2 tsp vanilla extract
1 tsp white vinegar
2 tsp cornflour

For the cream:
500g (2 cups) mascarpone
2 tsp caster sugar

For the fruit:
300g (2 cups) raspberries
300g (2 cups) loganberries
100g (½ cup) caster sugar
Splash of orange blossom water
Icing sugar, for rolling and dusting

1. Preheat the oven to 140°C fan/160°C/325°F/gas mark 3. Grease and line a 20×30cm (8×12in) Swiss roll tin with baking paper, coming right up the sides.

2. Put the egg whites in a spotlessly clean mixing bowl, and whisk to soft peaks. Add the caster sugar a tablespoon at a time, with the whisk running, until all the sugar is incorporated and you have soft, glossy peaks. Fold in the vanilla extract, vinegar and cornflour. Spread into the prepared tin and bake for 30 minutes until it has formed a crust on the surface.

3. While the meringue is baking, whip the mascarpone in a large bowl with the sugar and set aside. Then toss the berries in another bowl with the sugar and orange blossom water. Set aside as well.

4. Transfer the cooled meringue (crisp-side down) from the tin onto a work surface lined with a clean tea towel dusted with a good amount of icing sugar. Carefully peel off the baking paper and dust liberally with icing sugar. Use the tea towel to roll the meringue up into a scroll. This is to create a 'memory' in the meringue to avoid unwanted cracks later.

5. Unroll the meringue and spread with the cream, leaving a small border around the edge. Top with the berries and roll tightly away from yourself. Carefully transfer to a serving platter (I like to use a tart tin base for this), seam-side down. Dust with a final layer of icing sugar and serve. This could also be chilled for a couple of hours before serving but will need another dusting of icing sugar before serving.

AFTER a MEAL

AFTER a MEAL

BROWN BUTTER
WHITE PEACH CAKE

An easy cake for lazy summer evenings.
The browned butter gives it a nutty flavour
that I love. Serve with any of the ice creams
in this book or with a classic vanilla.

Serves 6

For the fruit:
5–6 large ripe white peaches, stoned
    and sliced into eighths
100g (½ cup) caster sugar
Zest and juice of 1 lemon

For the batter:
105g (¾ cup) plain flour
⅛ tsp salt
2 tsp baking powder
100g (½ cup) sugar
180g (¾ cup) whole milk
115g (1 stick or ½ cup) butter

Ice cream or cream, to serve

1. Preheat the oven to 170°C fan/190°C/
   375°F/gas mark 5 and line a baking sheet
   with baking paper.

2. Mix the sliced peaches with the sugar,
   lemon zest and juice and set aside
   to macerate.

3. Next make the batter. Whisk together
   the flour, salt, baking powder and sugar.
   Make a well in the middle and slowly
   whisk in the milk.

4. Brown the butter in a small saucepan and
   then pour into a 20×20×5cm (8×8×2in)
   non-reactive (not aluminium) roasting tin
   or oval baking dish. Pour the batter over
   the melted butter – do not stir.

5. Carefully spoon the sliced peaches over
   the batter along with any juices in the
   bottom of the dish. Place the baking dish
   on the lined baking sheet before placing
   onto the middle shelf of the oven (the
   lined baking sheet is there to catch any
   drips). Bake for 45 minutes–1 hour; the
   batter should puff up around the peaches
   and the edges should be treacly and
   golden. Serve with ice cream or cream,
   as desired.

CHERRY CLAFOUTIS

Clafoutis is a rustic French dessert of cherries baked in custard. Sometimes I make this with the pits still inside the cherries. Not out of laziness but because the almond flavour from the stones is said to infuse the custard. A safer way to do this would be to crack open a few of the stones and add the crushed *noyau* to the batter.

Serves 6–8

55g (¼ cup) butter
600g (1lb 5oz) cherries, pitted
70g (½ cup) plain flour
100g (½ cup) caster sugar, + 50g
    (¼ cup) for topping
⅛ tsp fine sea salt
3 eggs
300g (1¼ cups) whole milk
Cold double cream, to serve

Baker's tip: *Noyau* is the little kernel found inside apricots, peaches, plums and cherry stones. You can release these almond-shaped kernels by gently cracking open the stone or pit with a hammer. They are very intense and should be used very sparingly, but their bitter almond (the flavour of almond extract) notes are delicious added to custards and creams.

1. Preheat the oven to 170°C fan/190°C/ 375°F/gas mark 5.

2. Use 2 tablespoons of the butter to grease an oval baking dish about 23cm (9in) long. Fill with the cherries in a single layer.

3. Whisk together the flour, 100g (½ cup) of the caster sugar and the salt. Whisk in the eggs one by one and then the milk. Pour this mixture through a fine sieve over the cherries to remove any lumps.

4. Sprinkle liberally with the remaining 50g (¼ cup) caster sugar. Cut the remaining butter into tiny pieces and scatter over the top.

5. Bake for 40–45 minutes until puffed and golden. Let cool slightly before serving, with plenty of cold double cream.

RICE PUDDING
(GF)

Every kebab shop in my area of London sells a fairly good rice pudding, but the shops that have a wood-burning oven have the best because they bake their rice pudding in there and the tops are blistered and burnt in just the right way. I always ask for warm rice pudding, even though they are meant to cool and set. Eat yours warm or room temperature, whichever you prefer.

Serves 6–8

50g (3 tbsp) butter
75g (⅜ cup) caster sugar
100g (½ cup) pudding rice, or use
   risotto rice like Arborio
1 litre (4 cups) whole milk
1 vanilla pod
150g (½ cup + 2 tbsp) double cream
Pinch of salt
Drop of orange blossom water
   (optional)

1. Preheat the oven to 140°C fan/160°C/ 325°F/gas mark 3 and lightly butter a 20cm (8in) ovenproof dish.

2. Melt the butter in a heavy saucepan over a medium heat and add the sugar. Cook until it begins to brown, then add the rice and stir until the rice is coated and begins to get a little colour.

3. Next add the milk and vanilla pod and stir well. Add the cream and salt and bring to a simmer. Remove from the heat, remove the vanilla pod, stir in the orange blossom water (if using) and transfer to your prepared baking dish. Bake for 2 hours.

4. Allow to set for about 30 minutes before serving – or dive in while it's hot (like I do).

RASPBERRIES BAKED in MUSCAT SABAYON (GF)

Make sure to buy a good sweet wine as it is the basis of the flavour in this delicate dessert. It's super-fast to make but really can't be made ahead of time so pour your guests another drink, excuse yourself from the table and get to work. It should only take about 15 minutes all together.

Serves 4

8 tbsp Muscat wine (Beaumes de Venise or another sweet dessert wine such as Sauternes)
6 tbsp caster sugar
6 egg yolks
400g (2½ cups) raspberries

Baker's tip: Never leave egg yolks and sugar sitting in the same bowl before whisking as the acidity of the sugar can burn the yolks and make them grainy. Always combine the ingredients together just before whisking and then use straight away.

1. Get ready a medium-sized ovenproof gratin dish.

2. Pour the wine and half the sugar into a small heavy-based saucepan and heat gently until reduced by half. This should take about 10 minutes. Set aside but keep warm.

3. Place the egg yolks and remaining sugar in the bowl of a stand mixer and whisk until thick and leaving a ribbon trail. Remove from the mixer and then temper the egg yolks by adding just a few tablespoons of the warm wine mixture to the eggs and whisk-ing until smooth. Whisk in the remaining wine, being careful not to cook the eggs.

4. If your mixing bowl is heatproof you can use it for the next step; alter-natively, transfer the mixture to a heatproof bowl and place it over a small saucepan of barely simmering water, making sure the base of the bowl doesn't touch the water. Whisk until the mixture is beginning to thicken and is light and foamy. Meanwhile preheat the grill to high.

5. Pour into your gratin dish and scatter the raspberries over the top, then place under the hot grill for a couple of minutes to brown. Serve at once.

LONDON FLOWER FARMER: ORGANIC FLOWERS GROWN on an OLD FOOTBALL PITCH in EAST LONDON

At Violet, we decorate our cakes with flowers that grow near where we live and work, picked that morning, when possible. The London Flower Farmer next to the Walthamstow Marshes is one of the places we source flowers for our cakes at Violet. It's an urban location, but bleakly beautiful. Walthamstow and Hackney's tower blocks frame the view from the farm, where heritage roses and Café au Lait dahlias bloom in stark contrast. Treea Cracknell, who describes herself as a farmer-florist, is inspired by the seasons in much the same way I am in my baking. From late spring through to late autumn, we top as many cakes as possible with her flowers grown and chosen specifically for their colour and scent. Treea and I met at Spa Terminus market, where she sometimes sells her incredible flowers out of her sister's jam factory, England Preserves (which we also use at Violet). We started to chat, and it turned out her parents went on a roadtrip to California before she was born. They were so taken with the redwood trees they named their daughter Treea. Isn't that lovely?

Many of us grow a flower variety or two either in our gardens or in pots on a porch or terrace. When buying these plants, think about what might work on some of your cakes and desserts. The little Mexican daisies I have in the base of my pots make for sweet little embellishments on cupcakes. I also use the lemon blossom from my lemon tree, the purple flowers from my summer savoury, lavender or rose geranium. My mother grows incredible dahlias and decorates all of her cakes with them in the summer, so that is a great idea if you have more space. There is also a great farmer's market near me in Hackney where I can buy organic flowers for my bakes.

PARTY PARTY

BLACK FOREST GATEAU

In the 70s and 80s in Britain, this cake was THE thing on most restaurant dessert menus (or trolleys). It was considered chic and rather continental to serve it at your dinner party too. But my version is more like a chocolate and cherry Victoria sponge: springy chocolate cake sandwiched around a cherry compote with thickly whipped fresh cream. It's topped with an easy ganache and more fresh cherries and is perfect for outdoor dining.

Serves 8–10

200g (7oz) dark chocolate
185g (1¼ cups + 1 tbsp) plain flour
60g (½ cup + 1 tbsp) cocoa powder
½ tsp bicarbonate of soda
Pinch of salt
4 eggs
300g (1½ cups) caster sugar
150g (1 cup + 2 tbsp) vegetable oil
250g (1¼ cups) plain yoghurt

For the filling:
500g (1lb 2oz) fresh red or
    black cherries
4 tbsp brown sugar
4 tbsp cherry liqueur such
    as maraschino
500g (2 cups) double cream
2 tbsp caster sugar
2 tsp vanilla extract

For the top:
100g (3½oz) dark chocolate
    (70% cocoa solids)
120g (½ cup) double cream
100g (3½oz) cherries
Fresh flowers, to decorate (optional)

1. Preheat the oven to 160°C fan/180°C/ 350°F/gas mark 4. Line a deep 20cm (8in) springform cake tin with baking paper. If you don't have a deep tin you can use two shallower tins. This is a tall cake, so you are going for three or four nice layers of sponge if possible.

2. Melt the chocolate in a heatproof bowl set over a pot of barely simmering water, then leave to cool slightly. In another bowl, sift together the flour, cocoa powder and bicarbonate of soda.

3. Put the salt, eggs and sugar into the bowl of a stand mixer and whisk until very light and fluffy. With the whisk on a medium-low speed, drizzle in the oil, like you would for a mayonnaise, until all is incorporated and smooth and shiny. Fold in the cooled, melted chocolate, then fold in half of the dry ingredients then half of the yoghurt. Repeat, being careful not to overmix.

4. Pour into the lined tin and bake for 55–60 minutes. While the cakes are baking, make the cherry filling. Halve and pit the cherries and put them into a small saucepan along with the brown sugar and cherry liqueur. You can use a cherry stoner here for ease, but I still want you to cut the cherries in half for texture. Bring to a simmer and cook until most of the liquid is reduced and the cherries have softened, about 10 minutes. Set aside to cool.

5. Once the cakes are baked and cooled completely, remove from the tin or tins. If you have used one deep tin use a serrated knife to split the cake into three layers; if you have used two shallower tins split each cake into two layers (leaving you with four layers). Wash the cake tin and line it generously with clingfilm.

6. Loosely whip the cream with the sugar and vanilla and set aside.

7. Place one layer of the sponge into the bottom of the clingfilm-lined cake tin. Cover with a layer of cooked cherries and some of the juice. Cover with a layer of whipped cream, then place another layer of sponge on top and repeat the layers. Add the final cake layer and press gently to bring it all together. Chill for at least 30 minutes, or up to 3 hours.

8. For the topping, put the dark chocolate into a heatproof bowl. Heat the cream in a small saucepan and then pour over the chocolate. Let it rest for 5 minutes before stirring until smooth. Remove the cake from the tin and peel off the clingfilm. Resist the temptation to smooth out the cream, I like the impression left by the clingfilm. Place on a nice plate or cake stand and top with the chocolate ganache and more halved and pitted fresh cherries. Add fresh flowers (if using) and serve.

Originally created for my coeliac friend, the photographer Oliver Hadlee Pearch, for his 30th birthday, this cake has a pillowy gluten-free almond sponge topped with soft marshmallow meringue. While she was photographing this recipe, the inimitable Pia Riverola named it the Bubble Cake because of the shape of the icing. It stuck.

Serves up to 20

300g (2 cups + 2 tbsp) sorghum flour
300g (2 cups + 2 tbsp) brown rice flour
80g (⅔ cup) tapioca flour
2¼ tsp xanthan gum
2½ tbsp baking powder
75g (¾ cup) ground almonds
2¼ tsp fine sea salt
225g (2 cups) unsalted butter
750g (3¾ cups) caster sugar
120g (½ cup) oil
6 eggs
480g (2 cups) whole milk
1½ tbsp vanilla extract
3 tsp almond extract

For the marshmallow icing:
3 egg whites
150g (¾ cup) caster sugar
1½ tbsp golden syrup
Pinch of salt
1½ tbsp vanilla extract

Raspberries or loganberries and
  freeze-dried raspberry powder,
  to decorate

1. Preheat the oven to 150°C fan/170°C/ 340°F/gas mark 3½ and grease and line a deep 23×33cm (9×13in) rectangular tin that is 8cm (3in) deep.

2. Sift all of the flours, the xanthan gum and baking powder together into a bowl, then repeat, to be sure the flours are evenly combined. Then whisk in the ground almonds.

3. In the bowl of a stand mixer fitted with the paddle attachment, cream the salt, butter, sugar and oil together until light and fluffy. Add the eggs one at a time, beating well after each addition.

4. Pour the milk and vanilla and almond extracts into a jug and whisk together. Add half of the dry ingredients to the mixer and combine, then mix in half of the milk, then the remaining dry ingredients and finally the remaining milk mixture.

5. Pour the batter into the prepared tin and bake on the middle shelf of the oven for 60 minutes, or until golden and springy to touch. Allow to cool completely on a wire rack.

6. Once the cake is cooled, make the marsh-mallow icing. Put all of the ingredients into the metal or glass bowl of a stand mixer and place over a saucepan of boiling water (do not let the water touch the bottom of the bowl or it will cook the egg whites). Whisk continuously until the sugar dissolves and the mixture is very warm to the touch. If using a sugar thermometer, whisk continuously for 2 minutes, or until it reads 70–75°C (158– 167°F) – whichever comes first. Transfer the bowl to your mixer and whisk on high speed until you almost have stiff peaks.

7. Put the icing into a piping bag with a large round nozzle (or use a spoon) and pipe (or spoon) large blobs of icing onto the cooled cake. Decorate with fresh berries and a dusting of raspberry powder.

LEMON and ELDERFLOWER WEDDING CAKE

Much has been written about the creation of this cake for Prince Harry and Meghan Markle for their wedding in May 2018. But what I really want it to be remembered for is its delicate balance of sweet, bright lemons from the Amalfi coast of Italy and the heady fragrance of elderflower which permeates London's streets and country lanes at that time of year. We made the four large display cakes as well as enough bite-sized pieces of cake for 800 people to be served at the reception simultaneously, in the kitchens of Buckingham Palace. We later transported the cakes to Windsor Castle where my team and I assembled and decorated the enormous display cake on gilt cake stands from the Royal Collection. It was a dream job and a dream day. We got so much love and support for the flavour and design that broke from hundreds of years of fruitcake tradition. My California style of simple, seasonal baking suited the young couple's vision for the day and we made history, one layer at a time. All leftover cake was donated the following day to charity.

You'll need to make two batches of the icing but it's best to prepare one batch at a time, so just repeat the instructions to make a second batch in step 10. This cake is intermediate to advanced, not for the beginner!

Makes 1 large stacked cake,
to serve 30–40

For the curd:
3 eggs (about 170g)
8 egg yolks (about 160g)
240g (1 cup) freshly squeezed
    lemon juice
250g (1¼ cups) caster sugar
225g (2 sticks or 1 cup) unsalted butter,
    softened and cut into 1cm (½in) cubes

For the sponge:
800g (4 cups) caster sugar
8 eggs (about 440g)
1 tsp fine sea salt
800g (5½ cups + 2 tbsp) plain flour
3 tbsp baking powder
480g (2 cups) whole milk
160g (⅔ cup) vegetable oil
3 tbsp vanilla extract
160g (1½ sticks or ¾ cup) unsalted
    butter, melted

For each batch of buttercream:
215g egg whites (from 6 eggs)
350g (1¾ cups) caster sugar
¼ tsp salt
500g (2¼ cups) unsalted butter,
    softened
75g (5 tbsp) elderflower cordial

Fresh flowers, to decorate

Recommended tools:
Deep cake tins
Piping bag
Turntable
25cm (10in) cardboard cake board
15cm (6in) cardboard cake board
5 straws (not paper) or wooden dowels
    for stacking
Food thermometer

1. The curd can be made ahead of time and stored in the fridge for up to 3 days. Before making the curd, have ready a bowl or container fitted with a sieve. Weigh out the eggs and egg yolks into a bowl, whisk together and set aside.

2. Heat the lemon juice and caster sugar in a small saucepan until dissolved; allow to cool slightly. Temper the eggs by whisking a small amount of the lemon syrup into the eggs, keep going until you have added all the syrup. Return the mixture to the pan using a rubber spatula to get every last drop and cook over a low heat, whisking constantly until thickened. Once thick and coating the back of a spoon, remove from the heat and whisk in the softened butter, a few pieces at a time, until emulsified. Pour through the strainer and chill immediately.

3. To make the sponge, preheat the oven to 150°C fan/170°C/340°F/gas mark 3½. Grease and line two or three cake tins with baking paper: one 15×10cm (6×4in) and one 25×10cm (10×4in) cake tin.

4. In the bowl of a stand mixer, whisk together the caster sugar, eggs and salt until pale and frothy. In another large bowl, whisk together the flour and baking powder and set aside. In a third bowl or jug, combine the milk, oil and vanilla, then gradually whisk into the melted butter to avoid the butter seizing up.

5. Whisk the wet ingredients into the flour along with half of the sugar and egg mixture until smooth. Fold in the remaining sugar and egg mixture.

6. Pour the batter into your prepared tins and bake until the sponge is lightly golden, springs back to the touch, and a skewer inserted in the centre of one of the cakes comes out clean. The 15cm (6in) cake will need 35–40 minutes and the 25cm (10in) cake will need 50–60 minutes. Remove from the oven and allow to cool completely in the tins.

7. When the cakes are baking, make the first batch of buttercream. Whisk together the egg whites, caster sugar and salt in the bowl of your stand mixer (have your mixer ready and fitted with the whisk attachment). Set the bowl over a saucepan of simmering water and, using a balloon whisk, whisk the egg whites constantly, until they reach 72–75°C (161–167°F). If you don't have a thermometer, keep going

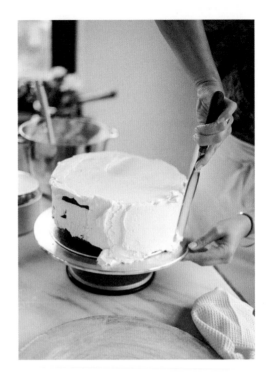

until the caster sugar has completely dissolved and the whites have begun to appear opaque. You can tell this by rubbing a small amount between two fingers. This should take about 10 minutes.

8. Once the whites are ready, remove them from the heat and immediately transfer the bowl to the mixer. Whisk on high speed until the whites have cooled and tripled in volume.

9. When the whites are whisked, turn the mixer speed down to medium and gradually add the butter, a little at a time, until it is all mixed in. The buttercream will split, but don't worry; it will come back together. With the motor on, gradually add the elderflower cordial. Turn the mixer off and scrape down the sides. Swap the whisk for the paddle attachment and beat once more until you have a smooth and fluffy buttercream. Place about half of the buttercream into a piping bag – no nozzle needed as this is just to build up the structure of the cake.

10. Split each cooled cake into three layers. This is best achieved using a serrated knife. If you have a turntable this is also useful for getting the most even layers. Wash out your cake tins and line them with clingfilm. Place one layer of the 25cm (10in) cake into its cake tin and one layer of the 15cm (6in) cake into its tin. Use the piping bag to pipe a dam around the perimeter of each of the sponges and then fill the centre with a 5mm (¼in) layer of the lemon curd. Pipe two stripes of the buttercream over this to create a little more stability to the cake. Place the next layer of sponge onto each of the cakes and repeat with the border of buttercream, lemon curd and stripes of buttercream. Top with the final layer of sponge and cover with the clingfilm. Chill the cakes for at least 1 hour or up to 24 hours. While the cakes are chilling, make the second batch of buttercream.

11. Place a small amount of buttercream onto the two cardboard rounds. Unwrap the chilled cakes and invert them onto their respective cardboard rounds. The buttercream works like a glue to keep the cakes on their boards. Now ice the top and sides of your chilled cakes. Place the 25cm (10in) cake on its cardboard round onto a serving platter or cake stand. Using the base of the 15cm (6in) cake tin, lightly trace a circle with the tip of a sharp knife or a cocktail stick in the middle of the larger cake. Push 4 of the wooden dowels or straws just inside the perimeter of the 15cm (6in) circle and the 5th dowel into the very centre of the 25cm (10in) cake until they are all the way down and making contact with the cardboard base. Lift the straws or dowels up slightly and trim them before pushing them back into the cake. You want them to be just beneath the surface. This is the architecture of your cake. Make sure they are as even as possible, then place the smaller cake on top of the larger one.

12. Decorate with fresh roses, peonies, hydrangea or other beautiful unsprayed flowers. The best are always the ones you can get from gardens, if possible.

PANDAN COCONUT CAKE with STRAWBERRIES

This cake was created by my former Head Pastry Chef Samantha Dixon and is based on a recipe her mother makes. This bright green chiffon cake is popular in South East Asia but can be found in the bakeries in London's Chinatown or anywhere there are South East Asian communities. There is a Vietnamese shop near me in Hackney that sells it. Some versions can be bland, but not Sam's, which is fluffy, bright green and filled with fruit and cream – you really taste the pandan and the coconut.

Makes a 20cm (8in) cake, to serve 8

For the sponge:
10 pandan leaves (or 5–6 drops of pandan extract)
4 egg yolks
100g (½ cup) caster sugar
¼ tsp fine sea salt
40g (3 tbsp) coconut milk
60g (¼ cup) vegetable oil
100g (¾ cup) plain flour
1 tsp baking powder
4 egg whites
¼ tsp cream of tartar

For the coconut mousse filling:
15g (½ oz) leaf gelatine
300g (1¼ cups) full-fat coconut milk
1 tbsp white rum
¼ tsp salt
400g (1¾ cups) double cream
1 tsp vanilla bean paste or extract
100g (¾ cup) icing sugar
400g (14oz) strawberries, plus 8 for top

150g (½ cup + 2 tbsp) double cream, to serve
1 tbsp icing sugar, for dusting

Baker's tip: Pandan leaf, also known as screwpine, has a grassy vanilla and coconut flavour. If you can't find fresh pandan, you can find the extract online.

1. Preheat the oven to 150°C fan/170°C/340°F/gas mark 3½.

2. Line the base of a 20×8cm (8×3in) round cake tin or springform tin with baking paper but don't grease the sides. You want the sponge to stick to the sides of the tin as it cools to keep it from collapsing.

3. Wash and trim the pandan leaves and put them into a blender with 120g (½ cup) water. Blitz to a purée, adding a little extra water if it is too thick. Strain the pandan paste through a piece of muslin, saving the liquid and discarding the leaf pulp. Set aside. If using pandan extract, add 5–6 drops to 120g (½ cup) water and set aside.

4. In the bowl of a stand mixer fitted with a whisk attachment, whisk the egg yolks with half the sugar and the salt until thick, pale and fluffy.

5. In another bowl, whisk together the coconut milk, 2 tablespoons of the pandan water and the vegetable oil and then fold this gently into the egg yolks. Transfer to a large bowl and whisk in the flour and baking powder.

6. Wash and dry the bowl and whisk attachment for your stand mixer. Whisk the egg whites with the cream of tartar until soft peaks form, then add the other half of the caster sugar a tablespoon at a time until glossy and stiff.

7. Gently fold the egg yolk mixture into the egg white mixture, then pour this into the prepared tin. Tap the tin to remove any large air bubbles and bake for 35–40 minutes, or until springy to touch. Tap the tin again when it comes out of the oven. Cool completely in the tin.

233

8. Once cool, run a knife around the edge of the tin and turn out onto a wire rack. Wash the tin and then line it with a large piece of clingfilm, with excess hanging over the sides. Then line the sides with strips of baking paper.

9. When the cake is completely cool, split in half horizontally with a serrated knife and put the bottom layer into the prepared lined tin.

10. Hull the strawberries (apart from the 8 for the top) and cut enough into halves to be arranged cut-side facing out around the edge of the cake tin. Use the rest of the whole strawberries to carry on in concentric circles until the sponge is covered, pressing them gently into the sponge so they won't move when you pour in the mousse.

11. To make the mousse, soak the leaf gelatine in some cold water in a bowl for about 10 minutes. Heat the coconut milk with the rum and salt in a small saucepan. Once hot, squeeze out the gelatine from the cold water and stir into the hot coconut milk until the gelatine has dissolved. Set aside to completely cool.

12. In a separate bowl, whisk together the double cream, vanilla and sugar until thick, but not stiff. Gently fold in the coconut milk/gelatine mixture. If the mousse is quite loose let it sit for 20 minutes to set a little and then pour this carefully over the strawberries. Smooth over, then top with the second layer of sponge. Cover with the over-hanging clingfilm and put in the fridge for 1–2 hours, or overnight.

13. When you are ready to serve, whip the double cream with the tablespoon of icing sugar until stiff, then pipe or spoon 8 dollops of cream round the edge of the cake (one for each slice). Top each dollop with a whole strawberry. Dust with icing sugar and serve.

ENGLAND

MOCHA BUTTERCREAM TIRAMISU CAKE

Tiramisu is arguably the most famous Italian dessert ever invented. It has many spin-offs because the flavour combination is perfectly balanced and we pastry chefs just can't stop ourselves from reinventing it in different shapes, sizes and medias over and over and over again. I created this cake version of the classic dessert by stacking layers of springy vanilla sponge soaked in espresso and brandy, filling it with mascarpone and covering it in a mocha buttercream.

Serves 8–10

For the sponge:
500g (2½ cups) caster sugar
165g (1½ sticks or ¾ cup)
   unsalted butter
80g (⅓ cup) oil
4 eggs (about 230g)
320g (1⅓ cup) milk
1 tbsp vanilla extract
500g (3½ cups + 1 tbsp) plain flour
1 tbsp baking powder
1½ tsp fine sea salt

For the coffee soak:
60g (¼ cup) water
60g (¼ cup) sugar
1 shot of espresso (about 4 tbsp)
2 tbsp Vecchia Romagna or another
   good brandy

For the mascarpone filling:
400g (1¾ cups) mascarpone cheese
240g (1 cup) double cream
60g (½ cup) icing sugar, sifted

For the mocha buttercream:
A little brewed espresso
6 egg whites
300g (1½ cups) caster sugar
300g (1¼ cups + 2 tbsp) softened
   unsalted butter
200g (7oz) dark chocolate, melted
Cocoa powder, for dusting

1. Preheat the oven to 150°C fan/170°C/ 340°F/gas mark 3½ and grease and line three 20cm (8in) cake tins.

2. In the bowl of a stand mixer, cream the sugar, butter and oil together until light and fluffy. Add the eggs one at a time, mixing after each addition.

3. Combine the milk and vanilla in a jug and set aside. Whisk the flour, baking powder and salt together in a bowl.

4. Add half of the dry flour mix to the mixer and combine, then add half of the milk mixture and mix again. Repeat with the remaining dry ingredients and milk mixture. Pour the batter evenly into the prepared tins and bake for 1 hour on the middle shelf. Allow the cakes to cool in the tins for a little while before turning onto a wire rack to cool completely.

5. While the cakes are in the oven make the coffee soak by putting all of the ingredients in a small saucepan. Bring to the boil, stirring constantly to dissolve the sugar. Once the sugar has dissolved, lower the heat and simmer for another few minutes, still stirring often. Transfer to a jug or container and set aside to allow it to come to room temperature.

6. Now make the mascarpone filling. Whisk all the ingredients together until fluffy, being careful not to overmix. Put in a piping bag and keep in the fridge until ready to use.

7. Now make the buttercream. Make the espresso and then set aside to cool. Put the egg whites and sugar into a heatproof bowl, then set this over a saucepan of simmering water, making sure the base of the bowl doesn't touch the water. Whisk continuously until frothy and all the

sugar is dissolved. Remove from the heat and, using a hand-held electric whisk, beat to a thick meringue until completely cooled. Whisk in the softened butter; it will curdle but then come back together. Add the melted chocolate and espresso and whisk to combine.

8. Wash and dry one cake tin and then line it with clingfilm with plenty overlapping the sides; set aside. Using a serrated knife (the longest one you have), score a horizontal line halfway up the side of each cake and then slowly cut the cakes in half horizontally. Slide a tart tin base or cardboard disc between the bottom and top layer of each cake, and lift off the top layer onto a large plate. Slide the bottom layer of sponge into the lined cake tin, drizzle the sponge with one third of the coffee soak and pipe a border of icing around the edge. Don't worry if the icing touches the clingfilm, as you are essentially creating a dam for the filling.

9. Now spread the mascarpone filling in the centre. Repeat the process with the second and third layers and then top with the fourth cake layer. Pull up the sides of the clingfilm and wrap up the cake. Chill for at least 2 hours, or overnight.

10. When you are ready to serve remove the cake from the tin and remove the clingfilm. Cover the top and sides with the mocha buttercream. Dust the top with a little cocoa powder. Serve immediately or keep at a cool room temperature until ready to serve.

SAVOURIES and HOLIDAY TREATS

BASIL, PARMESAN and PINE NUT SCONES

I love savoury scones. You can put just about any combination of cheese and herbs into a buttery scone and get great results. These are the perfect summer treat in a picnic. Frances and I have taken them as a snack to the Hackney Marshes not far from the bakery to forage wild blackberries. As with all my scones, you can make them and freeze them raw, then bake off as needed.

Makes 12 scones

400g (2¾ cups + 2 tbsp) plain flour, plus more for rolling
1 tbsp caster sugar
2½ tsp baking powder
½ tsp bicarbonate of soda
½ tsp salt
¼ tsp freshly ground black pepper
180g (¾ cup + 1 tbsp) unsalted butter, chilled, cut into cubes
1 egg
200g (¾ cup + 1 tbsp) sour cream
100g (3½oz) good fresh pesto (from a deli)
50g (1/3 cup) pine nuts
Freshly grated Parmesan
1 egg or egg yolk, beaten with a little water

1. Preheat the oven to 180°C fan/200°C/400°F/gas mark 6. Line a baking sheet with baking paper.

2. Put the flour, sugar, baking powder, bicarbonate of soda, salt and pepper into a bowl. Cut in the butter with a pastry cutter or a round-bladed knife (or use a food processor) until crumbly. Whisk the egg, sour cream and pesto together and add to the mix and stir in just to combine. Pat the dough into a cube and place on a lightly floured surface.

3. Let the dough rest for 5 minutes then flatten it to about 2.5cm (1in) thick with a rolling pin. Scatter the pine nuts over and then fold it in half like you are closing a book so that you have a rectangle, then fold it in half again so that you have a small square. Rest for 7 minutes and then roll into a square about 5cm (2in) thick. Use a sharp knife to cut the square into three long pieces. Cut each log into two and then each square into triangles. Chill in the fridge for about 30 minutes (at this point you can freeze the unbaked scones to bake another day).

4. Place the chilled scones on the lined baking sheet and brush with the egg and water mixture. Grate each scone with fresh Parmesan and bake for 25–30 minutes until golden. These are best eaten on the same day.

We add these to the Violet menu every Christmas. This is the same base recipe used for our famous cinnamon buns but with the cinnamon, sugar and cardamom replaced with paprika and blue cheese. They are excellent served as a snack with drinks.

Makes 12 buns

560g (2 cups) plain flour, plus more
    for rolling
2 tbsp baking powder
2 tsp fine sea salt
2 tsp paprika
250g (1 cup + 2 tsp) unsalted butter,
    chilled, cut into cubes
300g (1¼ cups) cold milk
50g (¼ cup) unsalted butter, plus
    a little extra for the pan
350g (12oz) Colston Bassett Stilton
    (or another good blue cheese)

For the eggwash:
1 egg
1 tbsp milk or cream

1. Preheat the oven to 180°C fan/200°C/ 400°F/gas mark 6 and butter a deep 12-cup muffin tray.

2. To make the dough, combine the flour, baking powder, salt and paprika with the 250g chilled cubed butter in the bowl of a stand mixer until you have a coarse meal. Slowly pour in the cold milk while the mixer is running, until the dough forms into a ball and comes away from the bowl. Turn the dough out onto a lightly floured surface and leave to rest for a few minutes. Fold the dough gently over itself once or twice to pull it all together. Let the dough rest a second time, for 10 minutes.

3. Melt the 50g (¼ cup) butter in a small saucepan and set aside.

4. Dust the worktop lightly with more flour and roll out the dough into a large rectangle until about 5mm (¼in) thick. Brush the surface of the dough with the melted butter and, before the butter hardens, crumble over the blue cheese.

5. Now roll up the dough, starting at the long side, keeping it neat and tight. Gently tug the dough towards you to get a taut roll while rolling away from you into a spiral. Once it's all rolled up, gently squeeze the roll to ensure it's the same thickness throughout. Use a sharp knife to cut the roll crossways into 12 even slices. Take a slice of the blue cheese roll, peel back about 5cm (2in) of the loose end of the pastry and fold it in back under the roll to loosely cover the bottom of the roll. Place in the muffin tray, flap side down. Repeat with the remaining slices.

6. Beat the egg and milk lightly together, then brush over the surface of the buns.

7. Bake the buns for 25 minutes. As soon as they're out of the oven, flip them out onto a wire rack, so that they don't stick to the tray.

SAVOURIES and HOLIDAY TREATS

I had only tasted mincemeat a couple of times before moving to London. It was in a pie brought to Thanksgiving by an intellectual friend of my parents who was visiting from out of town. The kids all turned their noses up and the parents politely took a sliver. But Dad always loved it, and if Dad tried it, so would I. In England everything changed. People are crazy for mince pies here. They are made as individual pies (which is quite cute) and served warm with mulled wine or brandy. At Violet during the holidays they sell out as soon as they are out of the oven.

Makes 12 mince pies

For the mincemeat:
125g (4oz) apples, peeled, cored
    and finely chopped
75g (3oz) sultanas (golden raisins)
60g (2½oz) candied mixed peel
100g (½ scant cup) apple juice
100g (3½oz) currants
Zest and juice of ½ lemon
Zest and juice of ½ orange
100g (generous ½ cup) dark
    brown sugar
½ tsp ground cinnamon
¼ tsp ground cloves
¼ tsp grated nutmeg
½ tsp fine sea salt
55g (½ stick) chilled unsalted butter,
    cut into very small pieces
2 tbsp brandy

For the pastry:
1 quantity of sweet crust pastry
    (see page 257)
1 egg
1 tbsp milk or cream

Baker's tip: The candied peel recipe from *The Violet Bakery Cookbook* can be used here too, if you want to make your own.

1. Make the mincemeat at least a day before you want to make mince pies.

2. Put the apples, raisins and mixed peel into a large, heavy-based saucepan with the apple juice, currants, lemon and orange zests (reserve the juice for later), brown sugar, spices and salt. Bring the mixture to a gentle simmer and stir occasionally for about 45 minutes/1 hour so that the fruit has started to soften and break down and the flavours meld together. Let the mixture cool slightly, then stir in the lemon and orange juices and brandy. Finally mix the cold butter through; it should melt a bit but not completely. Decant into a large jar or container and chill completely in the fridge until ready to use.

3. Remove the sweet crust pastry from the fridge about 10 minutes before rolling to soften slightly. Meanwhile, preheat the oven to 180°C fan/200°C/400°F/gas mark 6.

4. Grease a muffin or cupcake tray well. The drips from the filling can cause the pies to stick so this is a good safeguard. Roll the pastry out to a thickness of about 3mm (⅛in), then use a 9cm (3½in) round pastry cutter to cut 12 circles for the bottoms and a 6cm (2½in) cutter to cut 12 circles for the tops (gather up the offcuts and gently reroll until you have enough circles). Gently tuck the bases into the cupcake tray (no need to press into the tin firmly).

5. Fill the pies with the mincemeat (3–4 tablespoons per pie) and top with the pastry lids. (Any leftover mincemeat can be kept in the fridge for up to a month.)

6. Beat the egg with the milk or cream to make an egg wash, then brush this over the pies. Poke two holes in each pie with a sharp knife and bake for 20–25 minutes.

7. Cool slightly, dust with icing sugar and serve. They can also be served at room temperature and keep well for a week in an airtight container.

TRADITIONAL ENGLISH CHRISTMAS CAKE

At Violet we start making the Christmas cakes in August. The dried and candied fruits need a long time to soak in the alcohol to absorb the flavours and plump up. We also candy all our own peel which makes all the difference to the flavour. (You can find my candied peel recipe in *The Violet Bakery Cookbook*). You don't need to start as early as we do at the bakery but if you're feeling organised, start in November for the best results.

For the cake:
350g (12oz) raisins
350g (12oz) currants
150g (5½oz) mixed candied citrus
    peel (preferably homemade),
    finely chopped
90g (6 tbsp) brandy
140g (1 cup) plain flour
¼ tsp salt
¼ tsp freshly grated nutmeg
¼ tsp cloves
½ tsp mixed spice
50g (½ cup) ground almonds
Zest of 1 orange, plus 2 tbsp
    orange juice,
Zest of 1 lemon, plus 2 tbsp lemon juice
150g (1 cup + 2 tbsp) soft butter
150g (¾ cup) dark brown sugar
1 tsp molasses
3 eggs (165g)

To prepare the cake for icing:
60g (4 tbsp) brandy
250g (9oz) marzipan
3 tbsp marmalade or apricot jam

For the royal icing:
2 egg whites
Pinch of salt
375g (3 cups) icing sugar
3 tbsp lemon juice

23cm (9in) cardboard cake board
    (optional)

Baker's tip: Read this entire recipe all the way through before you begin (as I recommend with any recipe, but especially this one).

1. Soak the dried fruit and candied peel in the brandy and set aside for at least 2 weeks and up to 3 months. Stir the fruit every week.

2. The day you are going to bake the cake (at least a week before you want to serve it), grease and line a 23×8cm (9×3in) cake tin with a double layer of baking paper. Preheat the oven to 150°C fan/170°C/340°F/gas mark 3½.

3. Whisk all the dry ingredients together in a large bowl and set aside.

4. Add the fresh juice and zest to the soaked fruit and give this a good stir.

5. In the bowl of a stand mixer fitted with the paddle attachment, cream the soft butter, brown sugar and molasses together until light and fluffy. Add the eggs and mix well. Finally add the dry ingredients and mix until smooth, then fold in the dried fruits.

6. Scoop into your prepared tin and smooth the top with a spatula. Wrap another layer of baking paper around the outside of the cake tin by cutting a large square and setting the cake in the middle of it. Bring two of the sides up to meet at the top and fold them by creasing the paper and folding it down a couple of times to meet just above the cake tin. Then take the two opposite ends of the paper, fold them together like you would a package, and tuck them underneath. This creates a little tent at the top of the cake for the sponge to expand. You can tie a string around the perimeter to secure it if you like. Bake for 2½–3 hours, removing the baking paper after 2 hours. Use the skewer test here to make sure

SAVOURIES and HOLIDAY TREATS

it is fully cooked throughout – there should be just a few moist crumbs sticking to the skewer.

7. Allow to cool completely in the tin, preferably overnight. Use a skewer to poke the cake all over before drizzling with the 4 tablespoons of brandy. Cover with clingfilm or store in an airtight container (like a cake tin) for a couple of days or up to a week to let the cake mature.

8. Remove the cake from the tin and remove all the baking paper. Place the cake onto the cake board (if using); I prefer using one of these for ease but you can just use a plate. On a surface lightly dusted with icing sugar, roll out the marzipan large enough to cover the cake, working quickly so it doesn't dry out. Spread the marmalade or apricot jam over the surface and sides in a thin layer. Now lay the marzipan carefully over the top, smoothing it out to the edge and down the sides to the base of the cake. Trim away any excess marzipan so that you have a neatly covered cake. Leave to dry out overnight.

9. To make the royal icing, whip the egg whites and salt together until frothy, then add the sugar gradually. Add the lemon juice and beat until stiff peaks form. Spread over the top and sides of the cake in a nice thick layer. Decorate with more candied peel. Let the icing dry overnight before serving.

PASTRY DOUGHS

PIE DOUGH

A classic all-American pie pastry. Essentially this is a shortcrust pastry, like a pâte brisée, but it's the vinegar that gives it that signature diner flavour.

<u>Makes enough for 2 open-face pies, 1 top-and-bottom pie or 1 lattice pie</u>

375g (2¾ cups) plain flour
250g (2 sticks + 2 tbsp) unsalted butter, cold
1 tsp fine sea salt
6 tbsp iced water
2 tbsp cider vinegar

1. In a food processor, blend the flour, butter and salt together until it reaches a coarse meal texture.

2. Mix the water and vinegar in a jug, then add half of this to the flour mixture while the motor is running. Pulse a couple of times, then add the remaining liquid. The dough should hold together without being wet or sticky. Add more iced water only if really necessary.

3. Divide the dough into two balls and press into discs before wrapping in clingfilm.

4. Chill for at least 1 hour, or preferably overnight.

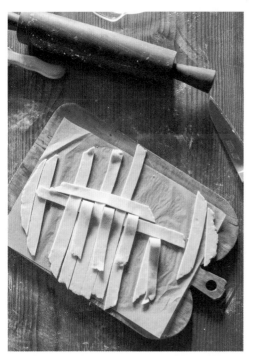
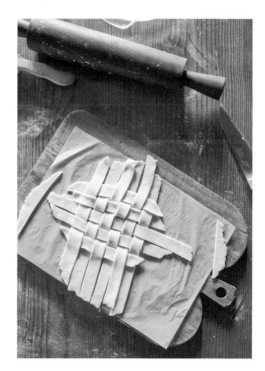

PUFF PASTRY

This recipe comes from the master Siew Chin. Making this dough is a bit like a meditation; it takes a LOT of time but it's about the process. The secret to Siew's perfect dough is how she tempers both the flour and the butter so that the two marry together so well. This recipe takes a couple of days.

Makes 2kg (5lb) dough:

Because it is so time-consuming you want to make enough for a couple of recipes and it's a nice size to work with. The extra dough freezes (rolled or unrolled) like a dream.

900g (2lb/4 cups) unsalted butter, cold
700g (5 cups) plain flour
4½ tsp fine sea salt
360g (1½ cups) iced water
1 tbsp lemon juice

1. Set aside 85g (3oz) of the butter and 85g (3oz) of the flour.

2. Cut the remaining butter into 1cm (½in) cubes and add to the bowl of a stand mixer fitted with the dough hook. Add the 85g (3oz) flour and mix until well incorporated – but you are not creaming the butter. You want to keep it as cold as possible and get it into a mass that you can form into a new, larger block.

3. Tip the butter onto a cold work surface (ideally a marble slab) and, using a bench scraper and a rolling pin, quickly roll the butter to a uniform 20cm (8in) square block, using the bench scraper to form even edges. Wrap the butter block in clingfilm and chill overnight in the fridge.

4. Put the remaining flour and the salt in the same bowl and add the reserved cold butter, cut into 1cm (½in) cubes. Fit the mixer with the paddle attachment and mix the butter into the flour until pow-dery, then change to a dough hook. Add the lemon juice and three-quarters of the cold water slowly, until just incorporated, continuing to add water until it forms a ball. Do not over mix.

5. Turn out the dough and gently knead until all the dry bits are mixed in, then form into a ball (the dough should feel moist and pliable but not too soft, even a bit rough on the surface). Using a knife cut an X on top, wrap in clingfilm and chill overnight in the fridge.

6. The next day, take out the dough and butter block and allow to come to tem-perature for about 10 minutes before rolling.

LOVE IS A PINK CAKE

7. Roll out the dough on a floured surface into a square that is about 28cm (11in), large enough to wrap the butter block. Place the butter block in the centre of the dough and fold each end over the butter to form a parcel. Pinch the seams to make sure the edges are sealed.

8. Brush off excess flour, then bash the square with a rolling pin in order to incorporate the butter into the dough.

9. Now the turns. Roll the square dough horizontally, to form a long rectangle about 5mm (¼in) in thickness. Tidy up the corners to form nice 90-degree angles, if possible. First turn: fold the dough into three parts, start by folding the right third over, then the left third. Make sure the edges are sealed, and stretch the corners if necessary to form 90-degree corners.

10. Second turn: repeat the above rolling and folding of the dough. Make a mark in the dough by sticking two fingers in one corner; this means the dough has been folded two times. Wrap the dough in clingfilm and chill in the fridge for at least 30 minutes before the next turns.

11. Puff pastry needs 6 turns, starting from the third turn. The dough needs to be chilled for 30 minutes after each turn until you get to the sixth turn. Mark the dough with 6 finger indentations, then wrap and chill the dough for at least 30 minutes or overnight before using.

12. Puff pastry can be stored for 3–4 days in the fridge or in the freezer for a couple of months.

LOVE IS A PINK CAKE

LARD PASTRY

This is a Southern American recipe that has an incredible flaky texture. The lard is essential – it makes the crispest layers but it lacks the flavour of butter, so the combo given here is ideal. It's great for fruit pies.

Makes enough for a top-and-bottom pie, or a large open-face pie

280g (2 cups) plain flour, plus more
    for rolling
¾ tsp fine sea salt
1 tsp caster sugar
150g (1 stick + 3 tbsp) unsalted butter,
    very cold
55g (2oz) lard
4–6 tbsp ice water

1. Add the flour, salt and sugar to a large bowl and mix to combine.

2. Cut in the cold butter and lard using a pastry cutter or a round-bladed knife. Add the water, a little at a time, and toss together with the knife or pastry cutter to bring it all together (you may not need all the water). If it still seems a little dry add another tablespoon of water.

3. Lightly flour a work surface and turn out the dough onto it. Use the ball of your hand to push the dough in a smearing motion, away from you. Do this a few times to incorporate the fat and water into the flour in a way that makes for a crisp and flaky pastry.

4. Rest the pastry in the fridge for 30 minutes before rolling.

5. This pastry can also be frozen for up to 3 months; just defrost in the fridge for a few hours before rolling.

SWEET CRUST PASTRY

This is the perfect pastry for tarts, where blind baking is required for, say, a filling of pastry cream and fresh fruits. This is the pastry we use for our mince pies at the bakery. It's perfect for cradling that rich, boozy and spicy filling and keeps well.

Makes enough for 12 mince pies or two large open-face tarts

360g (2½ cups + 1 tbsp) plain flour
¼ tsp fine sea salt
4 tbsp caster sugar
225g (2 sticks or 1 cup) chilled
    butter, cubed
4 egg yolks
4 tbsp iced water

1. In a food processor, mix the flour, salt and sugar and blitz once to combine. Add the cold butter cubes and blitz until the mixture resembles a coarse meal.

2. Add the eggs yolks and water and mix until just combined (about 30 seconds). Shape into a ball or cube and wrap tightly in clingfilm, then chill in the fridge for at least 1 hour (you can also keep this in the freezer for up to 2 months). Remove from the fridge about 10 minutes before rolling to allow to soften slightly.

ROUGH PUFF PASTRY

Rough puff is a quick way to get that flaky texture in your pastry. The flavour is amazing and this recipe works well for home baking. You will not get those flaky layers of true puff pastry but it's a great shortcut for the Tarte Tatin recipe (see page 69) if you haven't got the time or the inclination to make the real thing.

Makes about 1kg (2lb 4oz)

500g (2¼ cups) unsalted butter, cold
190g (¾ cup + 2 tsp) iced water
1 tsp lemon juice
280g (2 cups) plain flour
100g (¾ cup) bread flour
½ tsp fine sea salt

1. Cut the butter into 2cm (¾in) cubes and arrange them on a baking sheet, then put into the freezer. Add the lemon juice to the water and keep in the fridge.

2. In a stand mixer fitted with the paddle attachment, combine both flours with the salt. Add the chilled butter and mix on a low speed, just to knock off the corners of the cubes.

3. With the mixer running, drizzle in the water and lemon juice until the mixture just starts to come together as a raggedy dough.

4. Lay a piece of baking paper on your work surface, and turn out the dough onto it. Shape the dough into a block and roll to 38×25cm (15×10in). Fold in thirds, like a letter, then make an impression with your thumb at the top, cover loosely with clingfilm and chill for 20 minutes.

5. Repeat this four more times (five in total), resting for 20 minutes in between each roll and fold.

6. After the fifth turn, divide the dough into two blocks. Use right away or freeze until needed.

WHOLEMEAL GALETTE PASTRY

I love the flavours in so many of the wholemeal flours available now. Different varieties of wheat such as spelt or kamut, or even rye flour would all work well in this recipe. Think about the aromas in the flour and which fruits might suit it best when deciding which ones to pair together.

Makes 2 discs of pastry for 2 galettes

140g (1 cup) plain flour
130g (1 cup) wholemeal flour
Pinch of salt
Pinch of sugar
170g (1½ sticks) butter, cold, cut into
     1cm (½in) pieces
4 tbsp iced water

1. Combine the flours, salt and sugar in a bowl and cut in the cold butter with a pastry cutter or round-bladed knife. Avoid overmixing – leaving larger chunks of butter than you would think will make the pastry flakier.

2. Drizzle in the water and bring it all together into a ball, trying not to work the dough too much.

3. Wrap the ball in clingfilm, then flatten into a disc and let rest in the fridge for about 45 minutes.

INGREDIENT CONVERSIONS

Conversions are never exact. In certain places I have rounded up or down to make the conversions easier to achieve, e.g. a stick of butter is 113g but we round up to 115g in most recipes because few home scales calibrate single grams. But this is how I approach all baking and I want to encourage you to do the same – don't get hung up on a gram here or a gram there. Your baking will turn out beautifully by using these conversions below. And. If you don't have a scale, consider getting one. It's easier and more accurate. But then again, I do love a cup.

Oven temperature conversions

120°C fan/140°C	275°F	Gas mark 1
130°C fan/150°C	300°F	Gas mark 2
140°C fan/160°C	325°F	Gas mark 3
150°C fan/170°C	340°F	Gas mark 3½
160°C fan/180°C	350°F	Gas mark 4
170°C fan/190°C	375°F	Gas mark 5
180°C fan/200°C	400°F	Gas mark 6
200°C fan/220°C	425°F	Gas mark 7
210°C fan/230°C	450°F	Gas mark 8

BERRIES
¼ cup = 40g
½ cup = 80g
1 cup = 160g

BROWN SUGAR, UNPACKED
¼ cup = 45g
½ cup = 90g
1 cup = 180g

BUTTER
1 tbsp = 14g
¼ cup = 57g
½ cup = 113g
1 cup = 225g
2 cups = 450g
1 stick = 113g

CHOCOLATE
1oz = 28g
6oz = 175g
7oz = 200g
8oz = 225g

COCOA POWDER
¼ cup = 25g
½ cup = 50g
¾ cup = 75g
1 cup = 100g

DESICCATED COCONUT
¼ cup = 20g
½ cup = 40g
¾ cup = 60g
1 cup = 80g

EGGS
1 large egg = 60g
1 egg white = 40g
1 egg yolk = 18–20g

FLOUR
¼ cup = 35g
½ cup = 70g
1 cup = 140g
2 cups = 280g

GROUND NUTS
1 cup = 100g
½ cup = 50g

ICING SUGAR (powdered, confectioner's)
¼ cup = 32g
½ cup = 64g
1 cup = 125g
2 cups = 250g

LIQUIDS (water, milk, cream)
½ cup = 120g
1 cup = 240g

POTATO, CORN or TAPIOCA STARCH
¼ cup = 30g
⅓ cup = 40g
½ cup = 60g
⅔ cup = 80g
1 cup = 120g

SUGAR (caster, superfine, granulated and packed brown sugars)
¼ cup = 50g
½ cup = 100g
1 cup = 200g
2 cups = 400g

WHOLE NUTS
1 cup = 200g
½ cup = 100g

YOGHURT, SOUR CREAM, CRÈME FRAÎCHE
½ cup = 125g
1 cup = 250g

INDEX

A

almonds
    Bakewell Bars, 175–6
    Chocolate Almond Macaroon Teacakes, 155–6
    Fig Tartlets with Crushed Almond Frangipane, 11–12
    Triple Cream Amaretto Cheesecake, 79–80
    Wild Fennel and Roasted Fig Friands, 51–4
amaretto
    Fig Leaf Grilled Red Peaches, 189–90
    Triple Cream Amaretto Cheesecake, 79–80
apples
    Grape Slab Pie, 39–42
    Pink Apple, Lime and Bee Pollen Galette, 43–4
Apricot, Chamomile and Honey Scones, 161–2

B

Babka Buns, Chocolate Violet, 133–6
Bakewell Bars, 175–6
baking tins, xvii
bananas: Oasis Date Shake, 9–10
bars
    Bakewell Bars, 175–6
    Lemon Meringue Pie Bars, 55–8
basil
    Basil, Parmesan and Pine Nut Scones, 241–2
    Huckleberry Basil Sugar Scones, 13–14
Basque Cheesecake, 65–6
bee pollen: Pink Apple, Lime and Bee Pollen Galette, 43–4
Big Sur Cookies, 27–8
biscuits (American)
    Roasted Squash Cobbler, 103–4
    Whole Wheat American Biscuits, 15–16
    see also scones
Black Forest Gateau, 219–22
Black Tea Poppy Seed Muffins, 5–6
blackberries
    Blackberry and Chilli Pepper Pie, 37–8
    Blackberry and Rose Walnut Crumble Cake, 7–8
    Stacked Blackberry Jam Cake, 85–6
blackcurrants
    Blackcurrant and Violet Sorbet, 195–6
    Summer Pudding and Geranium Buns, 151–3
    Summer Pudding Sundae, 149–50
blanching, xvi
Blonde Peanut Butter Cookies, 29–30
Blondies, Grey Salt, White Chocolate Matcha, 59–60
Blue Cheese Buns, 243–4
blueberries
    Fluffy Blueberry Muffins, 121–2
    Huckleberry Basil Sugar Scones, 13–14
bread
    Cherry Tomato Focaccia, 99–100
    Whole Wheat Bread, 105–6
Brown Butter White Peach Cake, 203–4
Brown Sugar Victoria Sponge, 169–70
Brownies, Tahini Halva, 177–8
Bubble Cake, 223–4

LOVE IS A PINK CAKE

buns
Blue Cheese Buns, 243–4
Chocolate Violet Babka Buns, 133–6
Summer Pudding and Geranium Buns, 151–3
Butterscotch Puff-Puffs, 185–6

C

cakes
Black Forest Gateau, 219–22
Blackberry and Rose Walnut Crumble Cake, 7–8
Brown Butter White Peach Cake, 203–4
Brown Sugar Victoria Sponge, 169–70
Bubble Cake, 223–4
California Cake, 93–4
Chocolate Almond Macaroon Teacakes, 155–6
Chocolate Hazelnut Cake, 67–8
Chocolate Marshmallow Whoopie Pies, 159–60
Coconut Pudding Cake, 87–9
Coffee Walnut Cake with Fernet, 171–2
English Angel Cakes, 167–8
Jostaberry and Loganberry Matcha Cake, 173–4
Lemon and Elderflower Wedding Cake, 225–30
Marble Cake, 165–6
Mocha Buttercream Tiramisu Cake, 235–8
Pandan Coconut Cake with Strawberries, 231–4
Peaches and Cream Angel Food Cake, 63–4
Pistachio Green Plum Cake with Candied Violets, 47–8
Roasted Plum and Brown Sugar Buttercream Cake, 90–92
Stacked Blackberry Jam Cake, 85–6
Strawberry and Whitecurrant Coconut Meringue Cake, 163–4
Traditional English Christmas Cake, 247–9
Wild Fennel and Roasted Fig Friands, 51–4
Yellow Cake with Chocolate Frosting, 95–6
see also bars; blondies; brownies; cheesecakes; muffins
California Cake, 93–4
chamomile: Apricot, Chamomile and Honey Scones, 161–2
cheese
Basil, Parmesan and Pine Nut Scones, 241–2
Blue Cheese Buns, 243–4
cheesecakes
Basque Cheesecake, 65–6
Triple Cream Amaretto Cheesecake, 79–80
cherries
Bakewell Bars, 175–6
Black Forest Gateau, 219–22
Cherry Clafoutis, 205–6
Nectarine and Cherry Cobbler, 147–8
Cherry Tomato Focaccia, 99–100
chillies: Blackberry and Chilli Pepper Pie, 37–8
chocolate
Big Sur Cookies, 27–8
Black Forest Gateau, 219–22
Blonde Peanut Butter Cookies, 29–30
Chocolate Almond Macaroon Teacakes, 155–6
Chocolate Cream Puffs, 181–4
Chocolate Glazed Doughnuts, 130–32
Chocolate Hazelnut Cake, 67–8
Chocolate Marshmallow Whoopie Pies, 159–60
Chocolate Violet Babka Buns, 133–6
Double Chocolate Sea Salt Cookies, 157–8
Grey Salt, White Chocolate Matcha Blondies, 59–60
Marble Cake, 165–6

LOVE IS A PINK CAKE

ACKNOWLEDGEMENTS

Mom and Dad
Adam London
Adriana Caneva
Alex Porrata
Ali Schmidt
Alice Waters
Annabelle Lendrick
Cary Fukunaga
Claire Nitchman
Cynthia El Frenn
Damian Thomas
D'Anthony 'Goldlink' Carlos
Dakota Whitney
Emilien Crespo
Emily Martin
Ethel Brennan
Fanny Singer
Farmer Al
Felicity Blunt
Franco Fubini
Genesis Vallejo
Gilbert Pilgram
Greg Eastman
Graeme Hall
Henry Dimbleby
Ian Hundley
India Flint
Jaime Perlman
Jane Scotter
Janet Hankinson
JB Blunk Estate
Julie Engelschiøn

Kari Stuart
Karen Langley
Kenzo Caneva-Nishimoto
Kristin Perers
Lazuli Whitt
Maren Caruso
Mariah Nielson Blunk
Marianne Tatepo
Melanie Tortoroli
Mesa Refuge
Mireille Harper
Mustafa Ahmed
Nicole Bartolini
Oliver Hadlee Pearch
Penny Watson
Phoebe Von Reis
Pia Riverola
Rachel Colleen Boller
Rebecca Porrata
Robert Rodriguez
Ruthie Rogers
Samantha Kerch
SiewChinn Chin
Shiro Nishimoto
Skye Gyngell
Sue Chan
Susanna Hislop
Suzanne D'Coney
Sylvia Farago
Stevie King
The Duke and Duchess
    of Sussex

Tony and Laura Studley
Tom and Sherry Baty
Treea Cracknell
Yasmin Sewell
Yolanda Porrata
Whitman Shenk

All the Violettes
Alex Milne
Amanda Lind
Bethan Ecclestone
Charlotte Dupont
Christian Okunzuwa
Elizabeth Falconer
Emma Belabed
Fiona Fitzpatrick
Freya Thomas
Giulia Costa
Imogen Harvey
Izaak Adams
Jaehee Lee Gingell
Jules Larson
Louis Thompson
Mary Smith
Naomi Blair Gould
Niko Andreadis
Noa Farber
Paul Couve
Rory Brooks
Sam Dixon
Usama Seteha
Kap Rapoza

A California native, in 2005 Claire Ptak moved to London, where she opened the Violet Bakery in 2010. In 2018, she was commissioned to make the wedding cake for Prince Harry and Megan Markle's wedding cake. Before moving to London, Claire worked as a pastry chef for Alice Waters at Chez Panisse. Claire is also a food writer and stylist who has worked with Ottolenghi and Jamie Oliver, the latter of whom called her 'his favourite cake-maker in the whole world'. Her work has appeared in a wide array of publications including *Vogue, the Gentlewoman* and *the New York Times*. She has published four cookbooks before *Love is a Pink Cake: The Home-Made Sweet Shop, Leon: Happy Baking, The Whoopie Pie Book* and *The Violet Bakery Cookbook*.

First American Edition 2023

First published in the United Kingdom by
Square Peg in 2023

For information about permission to
reproduce selections from this book,
write to Permissions, W. W. Norton
& Company, Inc., 500 Fifth Avenue,
New York, NY 10110

For information about special
discounts for bulk purchases, please
contact W. W. Norton Special Sales at
specialsales@wwnorton.com or
800-233-4830

ISBN: 978-0-393-54111-3

W. W. Norton & Company, Inc.
500 Fifth Avenue, New York, N.Y. 10110
www.wwnorton.com

W. W. Norton & Company Ltd.
15 Carlisle Street, London W1D 3BS

1 2 3 4 5 6 7 8 9 0